Silently Silenced

Essays on the
Creation of Acquiescence in Modern Society

Thomas Mathiesen

Thomas Mathiesen is Professor of Sociology of Law at the University of Oslo. He was one of the founders of the Norwegian Association for Penal Reform. His many publications include *The Defences of the Weak* (Tavistock, 1965), *The Politics of Abolition* (Martin Robertson, 1974) and *Prison On Trial* (Second English edition, Waterside Press, 2000). Earlier versions of *Silently Silenced* have appeared in Norwegian, Swedish and German. This is the first English edition.

Silently Silenced
Essays on the Creation of Acquiescence in Modern Society

Thomas Mathiesen

Published 2004 by
WATERSIDE PRESS
Domum Road
Winchester S023 9NN

Telephone 01962 855567; UK Local-rate call 0845 2300 733
E-mail enquiries@ watersidepress.co.uk
Online bookstore www.watersidepress.co.uk

ISBN Paperback 1 904 380 158

Cataloguing-in-publication data A catalogue record for this book can be obtained from the British Library

Printing and binding Antony Rowe Ltd, Eastbourne

Cover design Waterside Press

Books in English by Thomas Mathiesen

The Defences of the Weak (Tavistock Publications, 1965)

Across the Boundaries of Organizations (Glendessary Press, 1971)

The Politics of Abolition (Martin Robertson and Universitetsforlaget/Wiley, 1974)

Law, Society and Political Action (Academic Press, 1980)

Prison on Trial (Sage Publications/Waterside Press, 1990/2000)

Silently Silenced (Waterside Press, 2004)

Silently Silenced

Essays on the
Creation of Acquiescence in Modern Society

Thomas Mathiesen

WATERSIDE PRESS

Preface to the English Edition, 2004

This book contains a number of essays on the general theme of silent and unnoticed political silencing which I largely wrote during 1977-1978. Most of the essays were collected in book form in Norwegian and published by Pax Forlag in 1978. At the beginning of the 1980s, the book was translated and published in Swedish and German. I translated the book myself into English in 1981, adding one essay that had not appeared in the Norwegian version, but left the manuscript unpublished in a drawer. I was too preoccupied with other matters.

However, the theme of how - silently and unnoticed - people are brought to silence, especially political silence, continued to haunt me over the years and decades. It seemed and seems to me to be a process which penetrates social life, notably also political life, in all its forms, certainly also in other Western societies like ours which have freedom of expression and democracy on the agenda. So, in 2003 I took the manuscript out of the drawer and had it typed into a computer. Thanks are due to Helga Smári Hanssen and Magnus Gommerud Nielsen for their painstaking accuracy.

The manuscript remained in my computer for a while. Then something happened in my own life which placed the process of silent silencing in bold relief for me. It was intensely political and intensely personal. I had never thought that silent silencing could have such a force in a person's life. In fact, I am silenced to the extent that I cannot write about it even now: maybe later if I live to be old enough. But I can say that what happened concerns the heart of what in Norwegian is called the 'care system', or 'aid system' (*hjelpeapparatet*). Ideally, the 'care system' is a part of the welfare system, and should in theory in different ways and through various institutions care for, help, support and provide treatment for people in various forms of distress, from psychiatric disorders to child welfare. However, in so far as it actually exists and is not a just a myth with symbolic functions for the welfare state, the 'care system' is *structured* in such a way that it silently and suavely makes clients and patients fall into silence, keep quiet, hold back their criticism, beware of protest, go along, be acquiescent and strategic.

But what happened at least jolted me to get the old manuscript up before me on the computer screen. It was a kind of vindication of the utmost importance of my concern with the topic.

This English translation includes all of the original essays which I had translated back in 1981. I have been tempted to augment, adapt and change the essays in line with events and developments since then. To a fair extent I have done so. The basic theoretical conceptualisation, with the emphasis on 'silent silencing', is new – in the original Norwegian version I discussed the issues in other terms that I now find less apt. Furthermore, in some of the essays I have deleted obviously obsolete material and added obviously clarifying passages, and also made a number of other changes. Other essays, however, largely remain as they were, the reason being that I think they are still relevant as they stand, only perhaps more so. But throughout the book I have added a large number of updating notes, many of them quite extensive, in which relevant theorising and empirical material as of 2004 are added to the essays. Taken as a whole and including the extensive notes, which I invite the reader to study, the book is in this way updated into our own century. Also, at the end of the book I have added two relatively short new essays, written in 2004 (*Chapter 8* and *Chapter 9*).

Let me be very clear on this: what follows is not at all a denial of the existence and, indeed, the expansion of types of repression which are very 'loud', visible and physical rather than silent and quiet. If I had denied that, I would have gone against much of what I have been working on, academically and politically, through many decades. Prison figures are soaring in many Western countries, police forces are expanding in terms of number of personnel as well as in terms of technological equipment and areas of control in society. The 'war against terrorism', which started back in the 1990s but acquired new impetus after 11 September 2001, has been loud indeed, with bombs and killings. It has involved vastly increased police and military activity, which in turn has had the erosion and downright downfall of civil rights in its wake.

This, however, does not detract from the importance of the silent methods of silencing people. Hidden in the deep structure of the expanding prison systems across the Western world various forms of silent and quiet structural forces are in operation, silencing criticism and protest against the prevailing expansive policy. The same goes for the police. Inside both of these sectors of criminal policy, there is uneasiness about what is going on, but the uneasiness rarely comes out, or, alternatively it is subdued to such an extent that thinking is more or less totally changed. And after September 11, with the stepping up of the war against terrorism, voices claiming that alternative roads against terrorism should be used, were clamped down upon – such as the idea of an alternative 'war' against *international poverty* which fosters terrorism. For example, at university campuses in the USA, criticisms of the way in which the war on terrorism was waged, were stifled. Observers from elsewhere have testified that critically oriented academics in the USA, who wanted alternative roads and who believed that the war against terrorism only enhanced terrorist activity, didn't dare to speak up, at least not loudly, or more or less changed their minds. To speak up would be more or less tantamount to treason. The American public system is an open and critical one, but apparently there are limits. The important thing here is that the methods of repressing alternative opinion were not noisy police methods and prison. Rather, they were largely silent ideological methods, including subtle forms of censorship. Deep inside academic workplaces across the nation, structural forces – especially power relations - shut many people's mouths.

The same thing happened after the war against Iraq got under way in 2003. Right before the onset of the war, there were loud international protests, also in the USA, and there have been protests throughout the war. But suave, silent and quiet methods of silencing protests against the use of the formidable war machine were employed to the utmost, in the media and in other ways. President George W. Bush's various sudden appearances among the American soldiers in the Iraq war, serving turkey on Thanksgiving Day and speaking as a tough leader on board a huge American warship, are cases in point, though in the light of Bush's peculiar kind of charisma they were not among the most silent and quiet ones. Bush's appearances were widely televised, bringing the message home not only to officers and rank and file soldiers, but to the public in general. It would require careful media research to find the specific effects of such appearances. But they were used as part of a vast battery of even more subtle ways, a wide range of censorious methods such as appeals to patriotism and duty to the nation as well as the importance of freedom and democracy which were presumably defended in the war, and so on. In line with this (and though other factors may also have been involved) the American opinion surveys for a long time showed a majority of the population supporting the war. On 20 March 2003, right after the military attack, 67 per cent approved of the job Bush was doing as President. Following the fall of Baghdad 73 per cent approved. Only then did the approval ratings start to decline, after among other things increasing coalition casualties and less victorious military results, down to 55 per cent in August 2003, a temporary boost but only back to 59 per cent after the capture of Saddam Hussein in December 2003, and further down to 51 per cent in March 2004 (CBS News Polls, March 2004). Later the approval ratings partly became still lower, the majority at times turning into a minority. The development has been similar in Britain, the other major country involved (and of course different in the other large countries of Europe, critical as they were from the outset). But we should note very clearly indeed that the minorities in the USA and Britain which in various ways supported the war and the occupation were still very substantial – despite casualties, exposure of the Americans' use of torture and so on, and, in the end, Bush won the election in November 2004.

In short, silent ways of silencing are often used in defence of the loud and noisy ones. Also, they may interact with the loud and noisy ones, and go hand in hand with them. Today, in this day and age of prisons, police and military activity (Bob Woodward has reported that when the war against Iraq was first contemplated in the late autumn of 2001, the United States' Defense Department had 68 – *sixty eight* – secret war and other contingency plans worldwide!) we tend to forget the silent ways of silencing in the clamour of the noisy ones. We need to be forcefully reminded of silent silencing in order to understand our political situation as a totality.

Silent ways of silencing are relevant today not only on the highest political level as mentioned above. The signals from this level trickle down to the lower levels of administration in the sector in question, and become authoritative signs to be followed there. As such authoritative signs, they appear and silence silently and 'as a matter of course', without crude methods such as batons and prisons: The political signals are simply to be taken for granted, and any doubts are to be set aside. As implied already, silent silencing is vitally important to the tens of thousands of people working in various branches of public administration – be they social workers, lawyers, health care workers, economists or general administrators. To give but one little example: In a Norwegian questionnaire study of lawyers working in public administration, 80 per cent of the respondents replied that 'correct law' 'at times' or more frequently has to give way to 'politically oriented assessments'. The feeling that politics overruns the work of lawyer as lawyers, and a rather resigned acceptance of this, is apparently widespread in public administration. Silent ways of silencing are equally important in the private sector, which is expanding in the Western world. Also here one little example: In a study of private court cases some years ago, I observed an insurance company suing a woman for fraud. She had twice lost a suitcase when travelling, and had claimed insurance both times. The company's lawyer tried to convince the court that the woman, who used high heeled shoes and had a rather dashing appearance, was an untrustworthy person. The company lost the case. When I called the lawyer afterwards, he forcefully stated that the case should never have been raised, and that it was an unreasonable and discriminating charge, but that he had simply done what was expected of him and that he had argued as best he could despite his doubts.

This book is perhaps especially relevant to silent silencing as it appears and operates over and against the wide range of professional and semi-professional civil servants and other workers in public administration and the private sector, including penal institutions of various kinds. An interest in punishment and penal institutions lies behind many of the theoretical notions presented in this book, and is the basis of many of the examples.

Please note clearly that what follows is not a denial of the fact that open criticism and protest exist in modern society. The last years' great protests and demonstrations against aspects of globalisation constitute a case in point. It may even be argued, as the Swedish researcher Stellan Vinthagen has done, that the globalisation - and peace movements - which are mobilised throughout the world today may involve more people than protests and demonstrations did during the 1970s. If I had denied that vocal criticism and protest exists, I would again have gone fundamentally against much of what I have been doing myself during most of my adult life, in areas such as criminal policy and political control. I am fundamentally an optimist as far as criticism and change go. What follows is, however, an ideal-type emphasis on the other side of the coin, the (silent) repression of protest, also necessary in order to understand our society.

Thomas Mathiesen
Oslo, November 2004

Silently Silenced

Essays on the Creation of Acquiescence in Modern Society

CONTENTS

1 Introduction

CHAPTER 1

Introduction

The Scandinavian societies have recently witnessed an increased sharpening of political conflicts and of 'the political climate' generally. A similar development has taken place on the European scene in general. A rather large category of politically active people on the 'Left' are being exposed to political repression. A wide circle of radical and critical groups is included.

To the Left, this is not necessarily a bad sign. The sharpening of political conflicts and measures means that the 'Left' has become politically more dangerous. Otherwise, it would not have to be persecuted.

However, two conditions are of considerable significance for the 'Left' if this development is not to *become* a bad sign. In the first place, it is important to *understand* the main features of the political repression which we are exposed to. Secondly, it is important to *organize* in order to meet the repression—against the background of an understanding of it.

This book deals with these two general themes. The book is a collection of essays. With the exception of this introduction, the chapters constitute essays which I have written on the two themes over the years, and which I have published in various professional and political contexts. As a consequence, the chapters are somewhat loosely knit together. On the other hand I hope that, taken together, they throw light on a relatively broad range of problems.

The two main themes of the collection—the understanding of the political repression which we are exposed to, and the significance of organizing in relation to it—need some further introductory comments.

By political 'silencing' is here meant attitudinal and behavioural subordination to political standpoints which are regarded as authoritative in the society or the group, so that acquiescence follows and given standpoints are accepted without protest. 'Silence' in this sense is a continuum, from silence despite disagreement (grudgingly you go along) to silence as an accepting attitude (you accept the standpoint, not even noticing that silencing has taken place, or at least not taking the fact of silencing seriously).

By 'silent' political silencing is meant that the bringing on of acquiescence takes place through a process which is quiet rather than noisy, hidden rather than open, unnoticed rather than noticeable, unseen rather than seen, non-physical rather than physical. In other words, a number of subtly different qualities are brought into the concept. Rather than going further into definitions, the subtle nuances will hopefully evolve from the text below.

In political debate and struggle, it is often taken for granted that in our late capitalist societies, the physical means of coercion which are the monopoly of the state—like the police and the prisons—constitute the most important methods of political silencing.

Obviously, the presence of physical means of coercion is significant, and quite obviously a strengthening—in terms of increased resources and personnel—is currently taking place, for example of the police and the prisons in many countries.[1]

At the same time, however, a one-sided emphasis on the physical means of coercion leads to a simplistic political analysis, and thereby to the danger of a poorly formulated political strategy. We are not only confronted by a state apparatus of physical coercion. Over and above this apparatus, which certainly may be and often is mobilised, we have a non-physical, non-violent—more or less invisible—type of political silencing to struggle against. The present book deals with this invisible or silent political silencing, which also constitutes a context for the use of the apparatus of physical coercion.

Let us first determine more closely the characteristics of the invisible, silent political silencing.

CHARACTERISTICS OF SILENT SILENCING

It is structural
The first distinguishing characteristic of the invisible, silent silencing—which sets it apart from the use of physical means of coercion—is that it is *structural*. It is the participants' position in a structure, in the relatively permanent relationship between units, which is silencing. A child welfare authority, for example, is silencing through structure—imagine the parent who refrains from criticizing the authority because criticism might make institutionalisation of the child, which is the issue, more likely. A series of similar examples from the Norwegian care system could be given. Because of your position in the structure, you have to act strategically—which means to keep quiet.

Structures are not immediately observable, but are derived from observations. The total pressure which stems from one's position in a structure thereby becomes correspondingly unobservable. In economic and political theory it has been emphasised that the basic structure of the capitalist mode of production itself results in invisible coercion of this kind. And not only in relation to the working class by the fact that its members have to sell their labour in order to survive as workers, but also in relation to the capitalist class by the fact that its members have to continue their maximising of profit in production in order to survive as capitalists.[2] But it is not 'only' the basic structure of the capitalist mode of production which has this invisible coercive character; so do structures deposited 'above' this basic structure, straight into the daily life of the majority of us.

---

[1] This was the case in 1978, when this book first appeared. But it was only the beginning. As of 2004 a great strengthening of the state's physical means of coercion has taken place, including a vastly increased use of police and prisons. Though there are variations across the Western world, the increased reliance on prison has taken place nearly everywhere. Contrary to popular opinion, it is to a large extent unrelated to the official crime rate. Rather, it is a matter of political choice. The leading countries are, of course, the US and Russia. The increased use of methods of physical coercion, however, does not detract from the importance of the silent kind of silencing discussed in this book.

[2] See Terje Rød Larsen, 'Makt og herredømme' (Power and Domination), *Sosiologi i dag* 1975.

An everyday matter

The second feature which characterises the silent silencing, in contrast to the use of physical means of coercion, is that it is an *everyday* matter. Remember that I am speaking of the Western industrialised world. Under our general social conditions, physical means of coercion are employed in situations of crisis, and toward marginal groups. I shall return to this. But our everyday life is not regulated by such methods. This has not always been the case: the feudal mode of production, prior to our own, was obviously strongly characterised by physical methods of coercion also in daily life, in the productive as well as in the private sphere. The emphasis on physical force was probably related to basic features of the feudal mode of production. Under the feudal mode of production the producers, the serfs, were not legal owners of means of production; nevertheless, they had certain marginal means in their possession: the piece of land which they literally stood on and were bound to, and which could be used by them for their own consumption. This possession of land made frequent use of violent means of compulsion necessary on the part of the feudal lord: violent force was necessary to enforce a work effort on the land of the feudal lord. The workers under capitalism, on the other hand, do not possess any means of production whatsoever for their own use—in order to survive, they are economically completely dependent on selling their labour to the capitalist on the labour market. Under such conditions, physical means of coercion become less important as routine methods—the purely economic compulsion which is built into production itself is, as the point of departure, sufficient to compel us to work under the conditions of those who purchase our labour.[3] Again we find this feature—silent silencing as an everyday type of coercion—to be not only part of the basic structure of production; we also find it characteristic of other social structures. And again, this does not mean that physical means of coercion are entirely absent and never used. They may be found and they are used, but in particular critical situations rather than in the routine of everyday life. The consequences of this for political analysis and struggle are considerable.

Unbounded

The third feature which characterises silent silencing is that it is *unbounded*. By 'unbounded' I mean that silencing is not a phenomenon which people may consciously perceive the limits of, and thereby keep at a distance from their own moral development. It is very difficult to pin-point the limits of silent silencing, you often do not know whether you are 'confronted by them' or not; in this sense they are fleeting or transparent. Thereby they easily 'corrode' you, corrupt you in relation to moral ideals which were your point of departure, and silence you. The open physical means of coercion will—this is my thesis—to a smaller extent have such an unbounded character. Though not necessarily delimited in full sharpness, they may at least be found toward the sharply defined end of the

---

[3]See Ernest Mandel, *Innledning til marxismens ekonomiska teori* (Introduction to Marxist Economic Theory), Bo Caverfors 1969 (Swedish edition) p. 35; Nicos Poulantzas, *Politisk makt och sosiala klasser* (Political Power and Social classes), Partisanförlag AB 1970 (Swedish edition) p. 24. A further discussion is also given in my book, *Law, Society and Political Action*, Academic Press 1980, chapter V. An addition as of 2004: This holds also under the conditions of the 2000s, with a dwindled (though not entirely absent) working class in the traditional sense, and a vast growth of service personnel , data experts and the like.

scale: the boundaries of the use of physical means of coercion may be observed, you know and feel when they strike you, you are conscious of them as striking you from the outside. By the same token they do not 'corrode' you in the same penetrating and intensely personal fashion as silent silencing does; they do not corrupt your basic moral ideals in the same unnoticeable way. And thereby they do not silence you in the same way: other things being equal, it is easier to initiate a struggle against an adversary who is using physical means of coercion (the use of such means makes the adversary themselves obvious) than against the unclear, fleeting, and progressive silencing of equal strength. We may observe this in specific areas of political struggle in our society, as for example in criminal policy: it is easier to muster consternation and resistance when representatives of the prison system clearly advocate a 'coercive line' than when the emphasis is on various 'soft' alternatives to imprisonment which are just as compulsive and just as silencing. Thus, it is more difficult to muster resistance for example against a psychiatric form of silencing than against the pure prison form. I believe the same to be the case on the general societal level: it is easier to muster broad resistance in a people against an unambiguous physical force than against silent silencing of comparable strength.[4]

Noiseless
The fourth feature which characterises silent silencing may probably be seen as a continuation of its unbounded character: in nature it is *noiseless*. By 'noiseless' I mean that the process of silencing takes place without the mobilisation of any particular apparatus, without any particular organizing from private quarters or from the state, and thereby without much public debate. Another way of putting it is to say that silent silencing is ingratiating or subtly invitational—there are, so to speak, no bells ringing to tell you that 'now the process of silencing is starting'. It is in the nature of the case that this contrasts with the situations in which physical means of coercion are employed. The latter are by nature noisy means: an apparatus, a particular organizing, which receives easy mention and attention in the mass media, must be mobilised. A prison strike may be quelled by dogs, clubs and guns—and reaches the mass media. In the Western public space of today, any sudden deviation from the routine of the everyday represents 'news' which must be given mention and is marketable. The mobilisation of an apparatus of physical means of force represents precisely such a deviation from the routine of the everyday.[5]

Dynamic
The fifth—and, here, the last—feature which characterises silent silencing is its *dynamic* character. By this is meant that the form of silencing develops over time

---

[4] The issue is probably more complex if we look at it in detail. For example, it is clearly conceivable that physical, violent coercion is to a marked degree paralysing when it reaches above a certain level—as for example in German concentration camps during World War II, or in dictatorial states outside the Western world. In the text above I have only dealt with the coercion/resistance relationship in gross and general terms, and in a Western context as of today. Addition in 2004: What I have said here must not be taken to mean that I 'prefer' physical coercion as a silencing method to silent silencing. It should be taken to mean that their consequences are different.

[5] The notions of 'noisy' and 'noiseless' silencing are taken from Mary-Ann Hedlund, 'Overvåkning—politisk disiplinering' (Surveillance—Political Silencing), *Hefte for kritisk juss* 1977.

and becomes, after it has received the status of a basic form of silencing in everyday life, continually more encompassing and continually stronger in its effect. Stated as a comprehensive historical generalisation: after structural political silencing has become the routine form under the capitalist mode of production following the feudal system, this form tends to develop and expand increasingly, becoming ever more encompassing and perfected in its mode of operation within society. Stated in still other words: what was at the dawn of the capitalist mode of production, several centuries ago, an unstable and highly vacillating transition to structural silencing, has increasingly—and especially in our own time—become the main form.

In his work on the history of the modern prison, Michel Foucault has in his way pointed to such development. He has attempted to show how the principles of the modern prison, which originated in Europe in the early 1800s, have later so to speak 'fermented' into society, where in a graduated form they characterise social life.[6] Here they more or less invisibly characterise large parts of the social fabric, *not* in the form of concrete physical prisons, but as silent principles of silencing. The development of society under capitalism may be seen as a development in a direction continually further into silent silencing. This implies that a main political emphasis from the political Left on unmasking and resisting the outspoken fascist political expressions which still exist, while important enough, does not hit the centre of the target. It is much more difficult, and in fact more important, to create political resistance against the softened fascism, in the form of silent silencing.[7]

The development which I am pointing to here is also mirrored inside parts of the development of the state's apparatus of physical coercion itself. I am thinking of the development of *the police*. As mentioned already, the last years have seen an increasing strengthening—in terms of resources and personnel—of the police in a number of late capitalist societies, and particularly of the physically coercive aspects of the police. But at the same time, increasing efforts are also being made to soften the clear and outright physical character of police control: 'local police' arrangements with a 'soft' and popular profile are being developed, in which the control of the police is presumed to be executed through close contact between a 'friendly' police force and the population. Arrangements for co-operation between police, schools and social workers are being developed; attempts are being made to develop and maintain the 'civilian' character of the police. Of course, this softening is not—and cannot be—perfect. And it is not necessarily and in all respects a bad sign that softening occurs. The essential point for our analysis here is that the attempt is being made. It means that far outside the boundaries of the structural and everyday silencing, attempts are made to leave the mark of structural and everyday silencing on the system of coercion. Under current social conditions, the closer they come to this mark, the easier it is to legitimise the methods of silencing. This is as far as it goes in relation to the police. As far as prisons are concerned, the situation is more unclear, but you do find tendencies in the same direction.[8]

---

[6] Michel Foucault, *Discipline and Punish,* Penguin 1977.

[7] To repeat: as of 2004, we see a resurrection of physical forms of silencing, notably prisons.

[8] In 1978 I predicted the same tendency for prisons as for the police—that is, a tendency to softening. As of 2004, with soaring prison figures and a punitive climate of public opinion, it seems less valid

In a sum: silent silencing, which is discussed in the essays in this book, is: structural; it is a part of our everyday life; it is unbounded and is therefore engraved upon us; it is noiseless and therefore passes by unnoticed; and it is dynamic in the sense that in our society it spreads and becomes continually more encompassing. The structural character of the silencing 'exempts' representatives of the state from responsibility for it, its everyday character makes it 'inescapable' from the point of view of those being silenced, its unbounded character makes it especially effective in relation to the individual, its noiseless character makes it easier to legitimise, and its dynamic character turns it into a mechanism of silencing which may be increasingly trusted.

In order not to be misunderstood, I emphasise again: this analysis is meant to hold for the development of political control within Western societies. And above all for the development of the most advanced of these—as our own. In other societies—also other capitalist societies—the relationship between open and hidden types of silencing and their effects will be a different one. The analysis which is given here will probably be rather poorly suited for example to the situation in many African states. But for we who live in Norway, and similar societies, it is important to understand the character of silencing as it has developed here.

To repeat, these are some general features which characterise what I have called silent silencing. But even though I have said that silent silencing is structural, everyday or routine, unbounded or diffuse, noiseless and continually spreading, I have not said so much about how silencing concretely takes place.

It is in the nature of the case that it is difficult to determine how silencing concretely takes place. Typically, such a determination would have been much easier if the issue had been physical coercion—which in fact it is not. In a way it may be said that silencing of the kind which is hidden is an insidious force in our social formation, and precisely as an insidious force it prevents political attention, consciousness and action around it from developing.

Nevertheless, something may of course be said about how silencing concretely occurs. This is what I am trying to do in the various essays which follow. Instead of giving a systematic account, I am trying to describe silencing as we see corners, bits and pieces of it in social life. And I am trying to describe silencing in accordance with the way in which my own thinking about it has developed. The more systematic description may then come later on. In other words, the essays in this book constitute working papers on the road toward such a systematic account.

---

for prisons. But the argument may still be made, at least for Norway, where prisons now have 'training programmes' led by prison officers, and where a proposal for converting one of the main closed prisons (Bergen prison) into a research-oriented 'university prison' (along the model of a university hospital) has recently (2003) come up. The 'training programmes' led by prison officers mainly have the function of providing officers with a meaningful task (inmates regularly view the programmes as something they must follow to get an early release), and the idea of a research-oriented 'university prison' will clearly function as a silencer of critical independent research.

THE WAYS OF SILENT SILENCING

By way of introduction, let me emphasise five main features which are typical of the ways in which silencing concretely takes place.

Absorption

In the first place, silent silencing—the structural, routine, unbounded, noiseless, and continually spreading silencing—in our society contains a strong element of what I would call *absorption* of attitudes and actions: attitudes and actions which, if they were supported on a mass basis, would transcend and threaten smaller or larger parts of the prevailing order.

In more detail, 'absorption' means that the attitudes and actions which in origin *are transcendent, are integrated in the prevailing order in such a way that dominant interests continue to be served.* This way, they are made unthreatening to the prevailing order. Absorption may be found as a significant strategy in large parts of industrial life: 'farsighted' businessmen become the carriers of messages which are 'ahead of their time', whereby potentially dangerous messages are absorbed. To mention but one example, in the commercial weekly press the hardest of businessmen become carriers of the viewpoint that support for women's liberation ought to be a part of the culture of the commercial weekly press.[9] But absorption as a strategy may also be found in state administration: administrators correspondingly become carriers of messages which have a 'future'. The absorbent ability of state administration has, in our society, increased through the years, and become an integrated part of the character of the state. Absorption of 'progressive' goals or purposes takes place: goals are given 'rounded edges' so that they are not threatening to the prevailing order, while simultaneously they are carried out in practice only to the extent that

---

[9]   As of 2004: This is by no means a strategy which belongs to the past. A case in point is the Disney Company which, in the light of the growing debate on gender, sex roles and the legitimacy of homosexuality, recently has released a film ('My Brother the Bear') which is supportive of such transformations. See Dag Øistein Endsjø, 'Skeivt i Disneyland' (Queer in Disneyland), *Klassekampen* 21 February 2004.

Also as of 2004: The essay referred to here (*Chapter 2 Silent Silencing*), relies on the commercial weekly press as a prime example showing how silent silencing takes place in private business. As intimated in the *Preface*, increased privatisation and market orientation, which are the orders of the day in the early 2000s, do not subdue the processes of silent silencing. On the contrary, they probably make them more pronounced. An example: In Norway, private economic interests have invaded state owned industry. For example, 24 per cent of shares in the Norwegian oil company Statoil are privately owned (the percentage may be increased to 33 per cent); and 46 per cent of shares in the Norwegian telecommunications company Telenor are privately owned (the percentage may be increased to 49 per cent). There are many other examples of parallel invasions. With reference to presumed successes in the UK and elsewhere, the Government is being advised by the global advisory company KPGM to allow private companies to build and run welfare service centres such as hospitals, schools, old people's homes and the like. The state in turn is being advised to lease these facilities on long-term contracts. Is silent silencing softened by such freedom of private enterprise? Probably on the contrary. As the head of Utdanningsgruppenes Hovedorganisasjon (the central staff organization for nurses, teachers, police officers and other educational groups) has pointed out (*Aftenposten* 19 August 2004), the increased business orientation of the public sector has reduced opportunities for employees to speak up publicly on professional issues. The reason, he says, is increased competition, which carries with it increased silence in public space.

criticism against the state is avoided. This development of the state has gone so far that we may probably speak of an 'absorbent state' in several highly industrialised capitalist societies in Europe. I have discussed the characteristics of 'the absorbent state' in some detail in another context;[10] in this book the phenomenon is discussed more briefly. The discussion may primarily be found in *Chapter 2*, which bears the title *Silent Silencing*. In that essay, the great development in the direction of absorption of transcending attitudes and actions is treated as a kind of 'crowning achievement', that is, as the last of a series of strategies used against threatening attitudes and actions in business life and state administration. Aspects of absorption, especially as they emanate from collaboration between certain private and state organizations and agencies, are also discussed in *Chapter 3, Silencing Through Pulverisation*.

System placement

Secondly, silent silencing contains a strong element of what I would call *system placement* of persons and groups which in origin represent attitudes, and a potential for action, which might have transcended and threatened the prevailing order. It is especially in work life that large groups are exposed to system placement and role assignment, thus subordinating people and so to speak grinding away at them; only the very few have a 'free' work situation. The subduing which the systems imply, prevents—just like the absorption discussed above—transcending attitudes and actions from developing: through system placement the individual is exposed to a long series of pressures which puts the brakes on transcendence. Max Weber pointed to something similar long ago, in his analysis of bureaucracy. The further implications and consequences of system placement are treated in *Chapter 4, System and Silencing*.

Professionalisation

In the third place, silent silencing contains a strong element of *professionalisation*. Persons and groups which otherwise might have represented transcending attitudes and a transcending potential for action, are sluiced or sucked *inter alia* into the large professions in our society, and no society brings forth professions which take a general revolutionary or basically critical stance. The subordination which professionalisation entails takes place during the training period: the individuals who are to become professionals must, through their years of study, expose themselves to series of conceptualisations within which they must operate if the examinations are to be passed and they are to *become* professionals. A particularly clear example of this may be found in the study of law. There, specific conceptualisations comprise a particular way of thinking which must be mastered—at least to a certain extent—if you are at all to become a jurist. But the same also holds for other professions. Furthermore, it is crucial to realise that the conceptualisations are gradually simply taken for granted, they become something which is not questioned or doubted, and they become, to the professional, a part of what the ethnomethodologists call 'common sense knowledge'.[11] But silencing does not only take place during the period of study itself. It also takes place in the work situations which professionals enter. The

---

[10] See my *Law, Society and Political Action*, Academic Press 1980, *Chapter 6*.
[11] See e.g. David Sudnow (ed.), *Studies in Social Interaction*, Free Press 1972.

professions grow large in phases in which the prevailing social order, with the prevailing structure of domination, needs them, and they attain—generally—a conserving function in relation to this structure of domination. This theme is treated in *Chapter 5, Sociology: A Disciplined Profession.* The essay ends in a discussion of the position of the sociologists, but examines their role against the background of the position of the large professions which have gone ahead of them—especially the lawyers and the economists.

Legalisation
In the fourth place, silent silencing contains a strong element of what I would call *legalisation.* In the chapter on the professions, mentioned above, I deal among other things with how new professions partly have taken over a hegemony which in the earliest phase of the capitalist social formation belonged to the lawyers. Nevertheless, the lawyers, and jurisprudence are still a highly significant disciplining element, and this is what I wish to emphasise here. More specifically, I wish to emphasise how law and jurisprudence have a disciplining function far outside the ranks of the legal profession itself. Very generally speaking, I believe one may say that jurisprudence, as a specific method of silencing others, contains two main components.

For one thing, the distinctive form of talk or presentation of lawyers constitutes a language of power which in itself has a strongly silencing effect on others. A crucial point is the emphasis of jurisprudence on the criteria of relevance, and by that token on the distinction, e.g. in court cases, between what falls 'inside' and what falls 'outside' a particular line of reasoning. This distinction, which also constitutes a main basis for the lawyers' conception of what is 'objective' or 'to the point', is related to refined sanctions in the legal culture: those who do not manage to see the distinction, or who think that the distinction is artificial, are sanctioned as standing apart from the intelligent as well as the good society. Thereby, the rest of us are either intimidated into refraining from opposition, for by opposing we may become outsiders, or we teach ourselves the language and stay inside. In both cases, our inclination to transcend in terms of attitude and action is subjugated.

Furthermore, jurisprudence contains a peculiar potential to transform political questions of conflict into apparently neutral, technical and professional questions—something which again silences the rest of us when confronting the questions. In parts this happens by the jurist's raising the fundamental legal question of whether there exists a 'legal authority' or 'legal basis' for given actions; in short, whether the actions are legal. Thereby the debate is transformed from being a clearly political debate—for and against a political standpoint—to being an exchange of opinions concerning the apparently neutral and unpolitical issue of whether legal authority or basis 'exists'. And partly the same thing happens with the jurist's raising the same question in a somewhat different wording: the question is raised of what 'the law in force' says about the issue under debate. Also through this formulation of the question, the debate is transformed from being a clearly political debate. In other words, the debate is 'lifted' from the political to the professional-juridical level, the professional-juridical level being regarded as superordinate and therefore more 'elevated'.

Parts of *Chapter 6* and all of *Chapter 7* deal with various aspects of this transformation from politics to apparently neutral jurisprudence—under the titles *Political Surveillance and the Public Arena* and *A Meeting of Judges in Italy—A Travel Account*.

Masking

In the fifth place, silent silencing contains a strong component of what may be called *masking*, that is, an outward change of name or shedding of skin over and above the legalisation process mentioned above. We have touched on the general process of masking earlier in this introduction—in connection with the dynamic, continually spreading, character of silent silencing. In this context I mentioned Foucault's analysis of the observable prison's tendency to 'ferment' into society, as a graduated and extenuated network of measures of (in my words) silent rather than observable silencing—very different from the prison, but nevertheless built on some of the same basic principles as the prison. In a brief *Chapter 8*, entitled *Panopticon and Synopticon as Silencing Systems*, I expand on Foucault's perspective by including not only the development of surveillance as he saw it, but also the mass media, as silent, quiet mechanisms of silencing.

Taken together: silent silencing is absorbent, system placing, professionalising, legalising, and masking in its silencing mode of operation. Through the absorption of goals which are threatening, the placement of persons or groups within system frameworks, professionalisation of problem solution in society, re-definition of problems to issues of law and a general masking of them, we are subordinated and silenced in terms of attitudes and actions.

The question may be raised of whether we are ending up in a kind of progressive 'spiral of silence' in our society. In a brief concluding chapter I discuss this possibility, based on the German media-researcher Elisabeth Noelle-Neumann's work. I end on a brighter note.

PHYSICAL MEANS AND THE MARGINAL ZONE

At this point, it seems necessary to repeat something which was said by way of introduction: the emphasis here on silent silencing does not mean that the physical means of coercion are eradicated as a state mode of control in our society. I reiterate that for example the police are in fact being strengthened. And I repeat that even if concentrated attempts are being made—as noted above—at softening the 'sharp edges' of the physical means of coercion and at providing them with the mark of silent silencing, those attempts are not always successful. In other words, also in our highly industrialised late capitalist society the physical, often violent means of coercion stand out and should be recognised.

However, the use of such means may now be understood more properly, that is, against the background and in the context of what has been said about silent silencing. To repeat, the physical, violent means of coercion are employed in a 'marginal zone' in our society, that is, in particularly critical political conflicts, for example, in certain kinds of work conflicts, and toward marginal groups such as vagrants, drug addicts, a whole range of criminals and the like.

The number of critical political conflicts, as well as the number of marginal people, is presently increasing in our society. The unequivocally physical means of coercion may be employed without too great a difficulty in these areas of society *precisely because the structural, quiet silencing is what most people to such a great extent are exposed to in everyday life.* Therefore, the use of physical means of coercion in critical political conflicts and toward particular groups becomes, to those who at any time constitute the majority, more or less distant stories from another country. *To those who at any time constitute the majority, the above-mentioned use of physically coercive means in turn does not demand any special legitimisation, and may continue relatively unrestricted.* In other words: physically coercive means may—paradoxically—be employed with all the necessary strength precisely against the background of the silent silencing which is the main rule. An appeal of mercy to the majority which at any time is subjected to this main rule does not work. The appeal is not understood, is not believed, and does not penetrate, because it does not resonate with anything in the average person's own everyday situation. In still other words: a sharp division between the everyday and the marginal, a division through which strong political conflicts and expulsion into marginal positions are kept completely outside the everyday zone, makes the employment of coercive means possible precisely in the zone which has been separated out as marginal.

If the use of the physically coercive means changed, and penetrated into the routine of everyday life because the really critical work conflicts as well as the deviant phenomena became a part of the everyday—well, then the situation might be different. Then appeals to 'people in general' would work, precisely because they would relate to something in everyday life. There are signs of this occurring today, with increasing poverty and other social problems in major Western states. But we should note that the forms of silent silencing are under dynamic development, they become continually more extensive and more effective, *so that the division between the everyday and the marginal may be maintained even if the marginal field as such is being enlarged.* Representatives of big business and of the state clearly see the danger involved if this division is broken down, and actively seek to avoid such a breakdown. And as long as it is avoided, most of us are caught in a kind of pincer movement: either we are exposed to silent forms of silencing which do not provoke us to resistance, or we find ourselves in a political or social situation in which we receive little outside help against the physical forms of silencing which then are used against us. In both cases, our power of resistance is paralysed. And the prevailing order is maintained.[12]

---

[12] As of 2004: Today's supposedly 'organized' crime (such as the much publicised bank robbery and shoot-out 5 April 2004 in Stavanger (Norway), and today's professionally inspired terrorism (11 September 2001 in New York; 11 March 2004 in Madrid) only enhance the bifurcation between 'us' and 'them' in people's minds. The widescale use of police force against large, globally inspired demonstrations (such as the demonstration against the EU summit in Göteborg, Sweden 14-16 June 2001) is somewhat different, in that large numbers of 'ordinary people', just wanting to demonstrate against global power, are involved. In such situations, the possibility of a breakdown in the bifurcation between 'us' and 'them' is present. But as the American sociologist William Isaac Thomas once said: 'If men define the situation as real, it becomes real in its consequence': it is interesting to see the great efforts made by the relevant authorities to define all demonstrators as more or less violent outsiders, or even as terrorists. This is done through political statements as well as legislation: Legislation against terrorism is such that a wide range of demonstrators at political summits and so on may be included. See my essay 'The Rise of the Surveillant State in Times of Globalisation', in Colin Sumner (ed.): *Blackwell Companion to Criminology*, Blackwell Publishing 2004.

ORGANIZED POLITICAL OPPOSITION

Finally, in this introduction, let me emphasise the following:

It is especially difficult to create organized political opposition against the silent forms of silencing and the conditions which follow in their wake. To repeat, this is the core of the strength of silent silencing. It becomes correspondingly important to contribute to such organized opposition.

As suggested at the very beginning of this introduction, the essays which follow try to confront this issue as well. I conclude most of the essays with viewpoints on how one can and should create political resistance against political silencing. The collection of these and other viewpoints into a systematic discussion will be an important task for the future.[13]

A particular point should be emphasised in connection with the question of organizing. In relation to the individual, the various forms of silent silencing function by educating us to self-censorship. Through the main process which has been discussed above, we are trained to check ourselves, censure ourselves, in terms of political attitude and action. Thereby, large parts of the political control are left to people themselves, which is by far the simplest control from the point of view of capital and state. The control 'works of its own accord'.

Through the self-censorship which is created, the transformation of short-term goals to long-term and structure-transcending goals is impeded. Not all short-term 'reforms' contain a long-term 'revolutionising' potential. Thus, reforms which in origin are positive improvements of the prevailing order do not. But reforms which in origin are negatively abolishing of parts of the prevailing order do contain such a potential. I have dealt with the distinction between positively improving and negatively abolishing reforms elsewhere, though further future elaboration will also be necessary.[14] The point here is that through the self-censorship which we impose on ourselves, the silent forms of silencing prevent the revolutionising potential, contained in negatively abolishing short-term reforms, from developing. Put differently: our rebellion is cut off, we do not dare to move on.

In connection with the political organizing which is necessary against the silent forms of silencing, it is crucial to organize effectively so that the courage to work with and for the transformation of short-term to long-term and structure-transcending goals is maintained and strengthened.

It is not so that every and any organizing effort functions this way. Three basic principles must probably be followed. In the first place, organizing in the form of a continual, questioningly reflective development of goals and means is decisive. Organizing where formal structure, and formal voting on questions of goals and means, is brought up has a tendency to ossify. Secondly, organizing in the form of a continual development of limited goals into wider aims is necessary. Organizing in which boundaries are set in a definite and absolute way concerning how far one might move has a tendency to ossify. Thirdly, organizing in the form of a continual return to and maintenance of the goals which were the

---

[13] See my book *Makt og motmakt* (Power and Counterpower), Pax Forlag 1982.
[14] See my books *The Politics of Abolition*, Martin Robertson 1974, and *Law, Society and Political Action*, Academic Press 1980.

point of departure, is at the same time also necessary. Organizing in which such a continual return and maintenance is not kept up alongside the movement toward wider aims has a tendency to ossify.

In other words: a structural-transcending organizing must be living and unfinished in the sense that it must be in a continual questioning development, and in the sense that it must give in to escape neither into short-term goals alone nor into long-term perspectives only. Only then do we have a chance to break also with silent silencing.

2   Silent Silencing

CHAPTER 2

Silent Silencing

One evening some years ago Norwegian television took up the question of the weekly magazines and the weekly press in the mass media. The background to the programme was the increasing significance of foreign property interests in the Norwegian weekly press. Participating was, among others, the managing director of Norway's largest group of companies in the field, called *Hjemmet* ('The Home'), which was under Danish ownership. During the debate, which lasted for a good hour, the managing director made several lengthy statements of principle and practice. Among other things, he emphasised two circumstances as especially important.

In the first place, according to him, it was important to emphasise that the Danish proprietors did not influence the selection and treatment of subjects and material in the magazines. The reason for this, he said, was that in fact the magazines followed a correct and sensible editorial policy in advance. And as long as this was the case, the ownership interests would not get involved; as long as this was the case, the magazines were allowed to do what they wanted.

Secondly, it was in his opinion important to understand that the readers—the public—wanted the kinds of material which the magazines presented. Without using precisely these words, he expressed the opinion that 'democracy' ruled in the trade: the actual fact was that the people wanted what the magazines gave them. During the programme, he was supported by some readers who said they liked to read weekly magazines.

The views of the managing director were not the only views which were in focus during the TV debate in question. But they constituted an important part of the general impression given by the debate to the viewers. And his views remained almost unchallenged. Someone else on the panel asked whether it was not the case that the weekly magazines focused on individuals without considering their economic and social background. To this important question the managing director simply replied, 'No'. This representative of the Danish-owned magazines undoubtedly appeared as the main victor in the discussion.

ORGANIZATION IN 'LINKS'

The statements of the weekly press representative, and especially the two main points mentioned above, are of considerable interest for an understanding of the way in which significant media function in our society. In more detail, the man gave—no doubt without knowing it—a good example of what may be called 'silent silencing' as it occurs within the structure of the media in particular and in social institutions in general. 'Silent silencing' functions precisely in this way:

The mass media, and other social institutions, are organized in 'links' which are chained together. Ownership interests (for example, those in control of capital in the mass media) allow given actions in the subsequent links in the chain (for example the journalists in the mass media), but only on certain conditions. These conditions generally have two significant features. In the first place, they are *tacit* or unspoken: they are—at least to a great extent, if not exclusively—unwritten and even rarely expressed verbally. They are articulated only when the next link in the chain goes beyond the conditions and breaks a tacit rule. Secondly, they are *broad*: they give considerable independence to the next link in the chain as long as the basic conditions themselves are upheld. These basic conditions may be of a moral or a political character, and they may— when the issue is economic ownership interests—be of an economic kind. In the context of the weekly press the basic condition is profit: as long as the profit is good, the magazines and their journalists are allowed to 'do what they want'.

'Freedom'
This in itself provides a point of departure for the formulation of an ideology which emphasises the freedom of action in social institutions, certainly including the mass media; that is, their opportunity to choose independently and ostensibly without external influence or pressure between alternative courses of action. Such an ideology is then consolidated when the tacit conditions are in fact *upheld* by the next link in the chain; that is, when the next link subordinates itself in advance to the same basic conditions. To the extent that the basic conditions— for example the condition of profit in the trade we are discussing here—are tacit or unspoken, no one takes them up. It is unnecessary to take them up. To all appearances, on the surface, your position is entirely 'free'. This is obviously what made the managing director of the Danish-owned group of weekly magazines emphasise so strongly the first point we highlighted from the TV debate, the point that his weekly magazines 'did what they wanted', and that no one, not even the owners, interfered with the work of the magazines. His magazines were adapted or subjugated, in advance, to the basic condition or the premise of the owners: profit. Such is the nature of 'freedom' in our expanding market- and profit-oriented society.

In an interview in a daily newspaper some time later, the same managing director elaborated on this point when answering the following question from a newspaper journalist, 'To what extent does foreign ownership influence editorial policy?' He replied, 'We are entirely free. No outsiders have any influence whatsoever on our editorial policies or on our correspondents. Our journalists travel anywhere and write about anything, the only demand we place on them, is that what they write about should concern people'. Only when asked, 'Such freedom is of course based on the condition that you make products which sell?' did he answer: 'Obviously. If we suddenly stood on the brink of bankruptcy, we wouldn't have our jobs for long. That holds for the editors as well as for me … We carry on in order to make money so that we can invest and secure our workplaces. This is our foremost task. If we do not manage this, we must be replaced by others who can do the job'.

This last question from the journalist, however, was formulated so as to indicate that it concerned something to be taken completely for granted—see the wording of the question—and so, in fact, was the reply. This was not to be reckoned as any kind of 'influence' on the group of magazines. In fact, the interview as whole carried the main headline 'No Foreign Influence on "The Two

Greats"'. The other of 'the two greats' to which the paper referred was another Danish-owned group of weekly magazine companies (*Allers Familie-Journal A/S*). At the time of the interview, the latter group of companies was planning a new magazine and the paper asked: 'Is there reason to count on the Danish owner interests giving a green light to such an expensive project?' To this the managing director in question replied: 'Most certainly. Our board knows that the issues and proposals which we represent are very well prepared.' The Danish-dominated board could accept the plan, and let the group of companies 'do what they wanted' without interference, because the group in fact ahead of the time was already thoroughly subordinated to the conditions taken for granted by the board.

Short-term interests
But this is just one half of invisible or silent silencing—one half of silencing which gives the impression that no silencing actually takes place, one half of the silencing which makes it possible to maintain, *vis à vis* a broader public, that freedom reigns. The other half lies in a more detailed relationship with this very public, with the readers of the weekly magazines, with the voters electing political parties or whatever. It is a central feature of many social institutions that they appeal to the short-term interests of the 'public' without taking up, and without trying to develop a sense or feeling for, interests of a more long-term kind. 'The public', 'the people', are viewed as passive recipients of messages from the institutions, and these messages mainly concentrate on short-term interests. Underdeveloped as the perspectives on the long-term interests thereby remain, an apparent alliance between 'the people' and the institutions is allowed to emerge. And the representatives of the weekly press may stand up and refer to 'people' as wanting precisely what they write; the party politicians in Parliament may, correspondingly, say that precisely their decisions appeal to 'the people'. As long as people are not 'disturbed' by thoughts of a more long-term character, this circle functions perfectly. And a circle is really involved here, because the messages from the institutions—from the weekly magazines or from Parliament, or what have you—stimulate these short-term interests: they support and reinforce a demand for precisely the content of the messages which the institutions transmit.

Thereby the interests of the first link in the chain (for example the profit interest of the weekly magazines) may be maintained *without representatives of these interests having to intervene with the arrangements or dispositions of the next link in any concrete way, that is,* without any *visible and demonstrable* silencing of the next link taking place. The journalists in the weekly magazine (and for that matter in the daily press) appear to have complete freedom to write what they want. The Member of Parliament, or at least the party which he or she represents in Parliament, appears to be able to make his, her or its decisions in complete independence and without any orders from the outside. The actual silencing of opinions and actions which in fact continually takes place in the manner I have suggested, is *hidden both to the participants themselves and to the spectators*. No external orders, and certainly no police or noisy methods, are brought in. The surface is clean and shiny, we do not see the political silencing which in fact is there.

Because the surface is 'clean and shiny', neither can the behavioural sciences to any significant extent demonstrate any silencing. Social scientists may of course maintain that a total system consisting of original background interests (for example profit), executive links (for example the journalists in the weekly or daily press) and a broader 'public', has silencing both of attitudes and of action as a *function*. But to demonstrate this with regular empirical methods is difficult, perhaps impossible, because the empirical methods used in the *behavioural* sciences—particularly in the behavioural sciences—register external manifestations and co-variations. This is, in fact, one of main features of positivism—emphasised by thinkers as early as Auguste Comte (1798-1857) : it is the 'positive', projecting or protruding knowledge, the knowledge that 'shows itself', which is to be registered. Thereby it follows that not even the behavioural sciences are able to demonstrate the process of silencing which we are speaking of here. This may be seen with particular clarity in a number of studies of the effects of the mass media, in which a main conclusion seems to be that it is very difficult to say whether the mass media have any particular effect at all on attitudes and actions. The behavioural sciences may even be used as further support for the view that no silencing takes place in the chain consisting of background interests, executives, and recipients.

MAINTENANCE OF HIDDEN SILENCING

We stated above: 'As long as people are not "disturbed" by thoughts of a more long-term character, this circle functions perfectly'. What, however, happens if people in fact are 'disturbed' by thoughts of 'a more long-term character'? What, in other words, happens if the receiving link in the chain is somehow stimulated—either by deviant executives within the chain or by others outside it—to break with the short-term perspective which is the basis of the chain?

If this happens, background interests or executives in the chain first try to a maximum extent to maintain the hidden character of the silencing in the chain. Solutions are first sought which are such that *open or visible measures of silencing inside the chain do not have to be employed*. Let me mention five examples of such solutions which are often used, without saying that the five are exhaustive.

Individualisation
In the first place, the condition or the event which may 'disturb' by bringing about thoughts of a somewhat more long-term character is often *individualised*. Through individualisation, the condition or event is made into something unique, atypical, something which deviates from the regular pattern, and from which you cannot draw radical conclusions concerning a change of course. Individualisation may be employed whether the condition or event simply occurs, as for example a major industrial accident, or is actively brought up as a piece of news which is unmasking and disclosing, as for example an item of information concerning inhumane treatment of prisoners in a prison.

A concrete example concerning an industrial accident may be found in connection with an event on board the Statfjord A platform in the Norwegian oil exploration fields in the North Sea in February 1978. A fire broke out in one of the platform shafts or feet, and five workers were killed. *Arbeiderbladet*, the Norwegian social-democratic government's own main newspaper at the time, commented editorially on the event under the headline 'Tragedy in the North Sea'. The very headline itself to some extent gives the event the connotation of being something unusual, something you did not expect. (Because if you were continually anticipating a tragedy, you would not have initiated the activity in the first place.) The first sentences in the text of the editorial give further associations to the notion that something very unusual has happened, which for that reason does not have to lead to any (fundamental) change of course: 'With the accident on the Statfjord A platform, we are again struck by a tragic labour accident. This time five human lives were lost. Labour accidents always attract special attention'. The editorial does not maintain that the actual event was entirely unique—as a matter of fact, that would have been a rather difficult position—but it emphasises that such events 'always attract special attention'. The atypical and 'non-normal' aspect of the event is consequently rather prominent. The concept of 'accident' itself—which I used myself above, because it is a customary term—carries with it associations of the unique or at least the unusual and abnormal; associations of something which deviates from the usual pattern and is not causally integrated in it.

Normalisation
Secondly, the condition or the event which may 'disturb' by bringing about thoughts of a somewhat more long-term character, is often *normalised*. Normalisation here means that the event is made into something to be expected, something which is a necessary consequence of a given type of activity, and from which radical conclusions concerning a change of course for this reason cannot be drawn. The strategy of normalisation is the counterpart of the strategy of individualisation. But any contradiction between the two is only an apparent one: if they are applied simultaneously to the same event or condition, they complement each other. More precisely, the emphasis on the event as unique, special, outside the pattern, must not go so far that the event—if it in fact occurs several times—becomes dangerously inexplicable. If it does, questions concerning the background pattern will be raised on *that* basis, since the pattern regularly appears to produce such inexplicable events. Thus, it is advantageous *simultaneously* to normalise the event or condition as suggested above.

An example may again be found in the above-mentioned editorial in *Arbeiderbladet*, which continues its analysis as follows: 'It would hardly be correct to characterise this accident as a typical 'oil-accident'. It seems more like a regular labour accident in connection with dangerous work performed under difficult conditions. The work took place in a deep shaft—or leg as it is called on this type of platform. It is a difficult and risky place of work whether the shaft is out there in the North Sea or on land. From prior experience we know of several such accidents in connection with mining activity'. Normalisation of this kind is of course reassuring, and functions as a reassurance together with its counterpart—the individualisation which was emphasised in the earlier part of the editorial.

Co-optation

Thirdly, the condition or the event which may 'disturb' by bringing in thoughts of a somewhat more long-term character is often *co-opted*.[1] In more detail, as I conceive the process here, co-optation consists of emphasising that the condition or the event should be used as a point of departure for making further improvements of procedures which were all right earlier, but which may of course always be made better. By such an emphasis any criticism which may be raised is so to speak punctured, and any thought of a fundamental change of direction, over and above the improvement of procedures which may always be introduced, is subdued.

Again an example is provided by the above-mentioned editorial concerning the accident in the North Sea. Immediately following the sentences which I quoted earlier, the editorial continues by saying:

> when this is said [that is, after the accident has been so effectively normalised], it must be added that the North Sea in itself is an extreme workplace. We must therefore demand maximum security measures. So far nothing has appeared to indicate that the security rules which exist, and which have been assumed as sufficient, have not been followed. Since the accident nevertheless happened, a detailed review of the whole sequence of events will be necessary to find new and even better solutions for such events. In particular, it seems necessary to evaluate warning installations and the solutions which have been chosen for evacuation. It will probably be necessary immediately to find new and better routines in this area.

With this emphasis, the editorial weakens the criticism which might be raised, the criticism is co-opted. The thought that the oil extraction itself should be reduced or perhaps even terminated in view of all the dangers following in its wake (which include a large number of work accidents of this kind), thereby recedes into the background.

Superficial endorsement

Fourthly, the criticism which may be raised against a given condition or a given event is not infrequently counteracted by *superficial endorsement*. 'Superficial endorsement' occurs when the criticism is too strong just to be punctured through individualisation, normalisation or co-optation. It is expressed through thoughtful and responsible—judiciously formulated—agreement that something particular is the matter, and should be corrected. The distinction between co-optation and superficial endorsement is a matter of degree.

Once more the above-mentioned editorial provides us with an example. Immediately following the co-opting sentences which were quoted above, the editorial continues as follows:

---

[1] Co-optation, from the Latin verb *cooptare*, meaning supplementary election of new members to a unit, performed by those who are already members; in Roman life, the filling up of the senate by the existing senators. The concept is widely used in sociology, meaning to include people hostile to a project in the project, thus making them co-responsible and thereby softening their criticism. Before World War II the sociologist Philip Selznick used the concept in his analysis of the Tennessee Valley Authority, inspired by the economic policies of President Franklin D. Roosevelt. See Philip Selznick: *TVA and the Grass Roots: A Study in the Sociology of Formal Organization*, University of California Press 1949.

In the report on the Bravo-accident [an uncontrolled blow-out in the North Sea in 1977], criticism was raised against the way in which the work on the platform was organized. There are indications to the effect that one should also look more closely at this side of the activity on the Statfjord A platform. Since it took so long to warn the main rescue station at Sola about the accident, one may suspect that those in command on the platform did not have a sufficiently clear view of what was going on at their workplace. To an outsider it does not seem very reassuring that a fire on board one of the installations in the North Sea does not immediately create full alert. In this we of course also include warnings to the rescue stations. Mobile, which is the operator on the platform, here has a responsibility which must be clarified.

Then follow some sentences which show the linkage between such endorsement of criticism and the above-mentioned co-optation of it: 'It should be added, however, that this aspect hardly has had any influence on the development of the tragedy Saturday night. However, it is an important point in order to secure better routines if an accident should occur again'. The 'co-optation' of the criticism emphasises 'better routines', generally better solutions, in order to prevent the consequences of events or conditions which are expected. The assumption is that the precautions which exist already, certainly functioned well in the case in point, but that they should be improved. 'Superficial endorsement' of the criticism emphasises in a carefully worded way that actual errors occurred.

Displacement of responsibility
In the fifth place, a *displacement of responsibility* occurs in cases when a criticisable condition has been exposed, or when a criticisable event has occurred, and when the criticism is so strong or so radical that it cannot be met just by individualisation, normalisation, co-optation or superficial endorsement. Displacement of responsibility implies that the responsibility in the area is in the near future to be placed on another agency or on other persons. Displacement of responsibility will presumably improve the conditions which are the focus of criticism. Such an emphasis takes 'the wind out of the sails' of the criticism: the new arrangement which is contemplated and to be installed is not tried out yet, it represents something new which cannot yet be criticised in terms of its consequences, and it is therefore difficult to continue pounding the criticism in. I am not asserting that such displacement of responsibility is always a purely tactical manoeuvre on the part of those responsible. In quite a few cases it is probably true that the reorganization was contemplated in advance, that is, independently of the event which has occurred. But the timing of the announcement of—or the renewed emphasis on—reorganization is hardly accidental even in such cases.

In connection with the above-mentioned accident on the platform in the North Sea, the oil minister immediately took steps and announced a displacement of responsibility which was to occur very shortly. The announcement was followed up in these words in our above-mentioned editorial in the government-supporting newspaper:

This case has also triggered a new debate concerning the responsibility of the control activities in the North Sea. Today this belongs to the Ministry of Oil and Energy and the Oil Directorate. It has been discussed for a long time whether it would not be more expedient, and also more correct in terms of principle, to transfer the responsibility to the Labour Control Department and the Ministry of Communal and Work Affairs. There is much evidence suggesting that such a change would be sensible.

And again we see how several of the various techniques are combined: the emphasis on reorganization of responsibility is followed up by some sentences which more or less emphasise co-optation of the event which is critised— sentences which also conclude the editorial as a whole:

We nevertheless believe that a close co-operative relationship should be developed in order to secure the utilisation of all expertise available in this field. It should also be emphasised, in connection with this discussion, that we here [that is, in connection with the various possible lines of responsibility] hardly find any part of the cause of the tragedy which now has struck us. Here as well, the question is how to find the best possible protection against future accidents.

In brief: individualisation, normalisation, co-optation, superficial endorsement and displacement of responsibility—all are strategies maintaining the *silent* character of silencing. All are strategies which prevent the last link in the chain, 'the public', from being disturbed by 'thoughts of a somewhat more long-term character', all are strategies which prevent the public from breaking with a short-term perspective. If more long-term perspectives appear and become significant to 'the public', visible and demonstrable measures will become necessary to maintain discipline. These are much more difficult to legitimise and defend.

*

Above we have taken as our point of departure conditions or events that to a greater or smaller degree demonstrate errors *or dangers in a given pattern*. If they are allowed to continue unchallenged by strategies of the kind we have mentioned, conditions or events of this kind make visible or even noisy measures of coercion necessary.

FULL-BLOWN ALTERNATIVES?

An entirely different kind of 'condition' or 'event' must, however, also be considered: the kind of 'condition' or 'event' which, rather than representing a greater or smaller demonstration of error or danger in a given pattern, represents a full-blown alternative to the given pattern. For example, instead of further escalation of the dangerous extraction of oil in the stormy northern Norwegian waters, it is possible to develop alternative sources of energy. From time to time the development of such alternative sources of energy is raised as a positive demand. And there are similar examples from other political contexts.

This kind of demonstration of, or demand for, goals which may be substituted for the given pattern, may also 'disturb the public' by eliciting 'thoughts of more long-term character'. The receiving link in the chain is, in other words, again stimulated to break with the short-term perspective which is the basis of the chain. If neutralising strategies are not employed, this may again make visible measures of coercion necessary to maintain discipline in the chain, whereby silencing is again transformed from being invisible to being more or less visible. However, once more various neutralising strategies exist which make concrete measures of coercion unnecessary and which thereby make continued invisibility possible. I shall mention five such basic strategies.

Construed as impossible
In the first place, the attainment of the alternative goal which may 'disturb the public' with thoughts of a more long-term character may be *construed as impossible*. It is maintained that it is not possible to carry out the suggested or demanded alternative goal without threatening or breaking down the general activity which was the point of departure. For example: when it is demanded, by organizations or persons, that films which are produced should deal with and mirror actual social problems which people confront in modern society, or when it is demanded that film should be politically relevant, the argument of impossibility is elicited: it is pointed out that it would be impossible to produce films of this kind with any reasonable guarantee of success; because there is no market for such films, and it would be damaging to the existing film industry. The main point here is that it is said in advance that people as a market—'the public'—prefer, and are receptive to, that type of film which is already being produced. This argument of impossibility invokes directly the existing market, and claims that the market—the voice of the public—makes the proposed reorganization impossible. We should note the connection which is built into the argument: the possible or conceivable change in 'the voice of the public' which a new type of film might contribute to is politically dangerous to existing film production. The very same potential change in 'the voice of the public' is simultaneously invoked as something which will not materialise, and as something which therefore construes the change which is demanded or proposed as impossible.

Construed as difficult
Secondly, the attainment of the alternative goal which may 'disturb the public' with thoughts of a more long-term character, is often *construed as difficult*. 'Construed as difficult' implies that the implementation of the change is not described as completely impossible. But the complicated, costly and rather risky nature of the implementation of alternative goals which are proposed or demanded is emphasised.

The transition from construing something as 'impossible' to construing it as 'difficult' is gradual and often imperceptible, and takes place when the alternative goal manages to obtain so much support that the former argument loses credibility. When this occurs, the change is not described as impossible, only very difficult to carry out in practice. For example: when organizations or individuals again demand that modern film should mirror people's real problems in our society, or that modern film should mirror politically relevant questions, and when such demands have grown so much in degree that they can no longer be rejected as entirely unfeasible on the above-mentioned grounds (people increasingly begin to show a certain interest for films of this kind), a transition is made to arguments construing a change of this kind as very difficult: the change becomes too complicated and costly, the reorganization is still after all risky because the interest in alternative film which is now beginning to appear may be temporary, etc. The arguments involving difficulties are mixed as much as possible with arguments stressing impossibilities, because one's position is much stronger when it may be said that 'people' simply do not 'want' the alternative goals and approaches: the arguments stressing the impossibility of change are the arguments which hit the opposition hardest; these are the arguments which most easily reduce the opposition to silence.

Construed as undesirable

Thirdly, the alternative goal is often *construed as undesirable.* Construing something as 'undesirable' implies that the implementation of the change which is demanded, is characterised neither as impossible nor difficult, but rather as distasteful and unwanted on the basis of given criteria, because the blessings involved in what already exists are thereby lost. Construing something as undesirable in other words involves a contrasting of the new values with the old, and an opening up of a debate concerning values: the superiority of the old values is contrasted with the new values.

For example: the suspense of the crime film, the entertainment of the Western, the presumed relaxation of the pornographic movie for the sexually timid, are presented as values and debated over and against the values built into the new kinds of film which are demanded. This step in the political struggle— the stage at which this strategy is added—implies an important partial victory for those demanding alternative goals. For example, for those who demand alternative film: at this stage, the defenders of the prevailing order have been put on the defensive, and the debate concerns what it always should concern: political values. Nevertheless the defence argument contains potential strengths: the suspense of the crime movie, the entertainment of the Western, the presumed sexual excitement or relaxation provided by the porno film, or whatever, all contain values which are indeed important to 'the public'. Put differently: these types of values may be satisfied in other ways in a more totally alternative society. But we are not yet even approaching such a society, so the traditional forms of satisfaction will still have their appeal. In addition, the strategy of construing alternative forms as undesirable is in practice combined with the preceding strategies—the strategies of construing something as difficult or (best from a defensive point of view) construing it as impossible—so that a complete arsenal of strategies for the maintenance of the prevailing order remains present.

Double-tracked

In the fourth place, old and new goals are not infrequently *double-tracked.* This implies that the activity in question is actually partly reorganized, so that both types of goals have a place within the activity—but with the old goals in the first priority. Such partial reorganization takes place when the pressure in the direction of the alternative goals becomes so great that arguments in the form of construing something as impossible, difficult or undesirable are no longer sufficient. Something must also 'be done' to satisfy the opposition. To give an example: 'alternative' film, for example highly politicised film, is given the opportunity to exist alongside traditional film, supported by some state funds (or private funds, donated by the sources which also finance traditional film) as a financial foundation. In other words, oppositional film too is given its 'share'.

This double-tracking has several important functions for the main activity— that is, for the traditional activity. Firstly, an impression is given of democratic 'space' for 'deviant' activities and opinions: a 'radical alibi' is secured. Secondly, opportunities are provided to substantiate assumptions about how dangerous a more total transformation to the alternative activity would be: the alternative activity in its *limited* form regularly proves to be unprofitable, or to be difficult to carry through. The fact that a more total transformation to the alternative activity might abolish these limitations, and thereby perhaps might make a profitable activity possible, is in this context usually not brought up. Under the seal of double-tracking, the alternative activity reveals its limitations against the background of the limited degrees of freedom in practice allowed to it. Traditional activity wins and is enabled to employ the arguments of the impossible, the difficult, and the undesirable over again, with renewed strength.

Absorbed

In the fifth place, the new goals are not infrequently *absorbed*. That is to say, the activity in question is reorganized not only sufficiently for the alternative goals to show themselves in a limited fashion, but in fact sufficiently for the alternative goals to become more or less the main thing, or one of the main things. This occurs when the pressure in the direction of the alternative goals has become so great and universal that even the four above-mentioned techniques are unable to curb it. But when it occurs, it takes place in a form which *integrates* the new goals into the old type of activity, so that the new goals begin to serve the interests which were promoted by the old goals. Integration into the old type of activity implies that the new type is sufficiently cut in the edges and polished so that it fits in without creating too much disturbance.

Let us use again our example from film: one begins to produce 'critical' film—cut in the edges and polished—not as a side activity and in the shadows of traditional film, but as a main type of film, at least as an equal partner to the traditional film. And it is produced because it now appears that this type of film too may be profitable in terms of economy, status, and in other ways. A market for it has, of course, been created.[2] Another example: the feminist goal of

---

[2]   I touch on 'absorption' in a more general way in *Chapter 1*. Another word for it is of course co-optation, which is used earlier in this chapter (see the preceding note). As of 2004: A very good example of absorption or co-optation in the film industry is the upsurge of films, in the present decade, about more or less man-made catastrophes. A particular and major political concern in our time is man-made pollution and even major disturbance of the environment. A radical critique of man-made disturbance of the environment is absorbed and transformed into a highly marketable and best selling film in the movie *The Day after Tomorrow* (2004). In this film a global increase in temperature suddenly creates a new ice age in the Northern hemisphere, having dire and dramatic consequences for the entire globe. A cataclysmic environmental change, literally from one day to another, is as far as we know extremely unlikely, but may occur over a longer span of time. However, a story like this, produced for the screen with all the modern digital effects, draws on the criticism of man-made environmental disturbances as well as on people's fears and fantasies, and is, to put it mildly, highly marketable.

women's liberation, liberation from traditional sex role patterns, is integrated as an important part of the goals of large parts of the popular weekly press which address women, because this is beginning to be profitable economically and in other ways. The transition from what we earlier called 'double-tracking' to 'absorption' is gradual, and 'absorption' may actually often be viewed as a type of 'double-tracking', but because a more or less total transition is in fact possible, I use the word 'absorption'.

In brief: construing something as impossible, construing it as difficult, construing it as undesirable, double-tracking and absorption—all are strategies to maintain the silent or hidden character of compulsion in the chain consisting of background interests, executive institutions and a public or audience which the executives address. All are strategies which prevent the last link in the chain—the public—from being disturbed by 'thoughts of a more long-term character' in which fully alternative arrangements and goals are demanded. In varying degrees the first strategies imply that the alternative and 'disturbing' arrangements and goals are kept at a distance—they are kept at a distance up to the point where this is no longer possible. Then the alternative arrangements and goals are simply taken over by being integrated into the ongoing activity in such a way that they serve the interests which stand behind the activity. They are absorbed.

It is important to understand how absorption simultaneously has another significant consequence: that of *making harmless the arrangements and goals which in origin might have 'disturbed' the public with thoughts of a more long-term character.* Precisely by being incorporated into the ongoing activity, the alternative issue does not cause such great 'alarm': the context of the ongoing activity lends a sufficient degree of respectability to the 'alternative'. The women's liberation movement absorbed into the UN's celebration of Women's Year is a case in point. An underlying assumption here is that the form of communication itself to a significant degree influences the reception of the content. In particular, I assume that when the content is enthusiastically taken up by someone to whom it should appear remote (e.g. the traditional weekly women's magazine beginning to discuss issues of women's liberation), this gives the impression that those who take up the content (e.g. the traditional weekly women's magazine) are undergoing fundamental change (that is, change of basic premises). Thereby the critique which was presented initially is softened or silenced: it appears less relevant. Actually, the change is not fundamental, actually the same background interests are served by the new development. But *the impression* of fundamental change is given, and critique is given more difficult terms.

*

American disaster movies in the 1950s built on people's fears of Communism, atom bombs, radioactive damage, and so on. Some of the criticism absorbed into these best-sellers was radical, but absorbed and transformed into best selling horror stories, such as stories about carnivorous insects becoming extremely large and dangerous animals through mutation following from nuclear radiation. Parallel American films in the 1970s portrayed—but never analysed—actual critical events such as the Vietnam War, the Watergate scandal, and so on. Almost invariably, they were provided with a happy ending.

Since absorption transforms a content, which otherwise might have 'disturbed' the public with thoughts of a more long-term character, into something harmless, it may be asked why absorption is not employed more directly—without the long road via the other strategies which have been discussed above. The answer is that in fact this does occur quite frequently. In the first place, it occurs in trade and industry: quite frequently 'farsighted' businessmen become the carriers of messages which are 'ahead of their time', for example carriers of the view that support for women's liberation issues should become a part of the culture of the commercial weekly press. We have alluded to this before. Secondly, it occurs in state administration: administrators likewise become carriers of messages which have 'a promising future'. But probably it has, at least until recently, occurred more frequently in business life than in state administration. There are several reasons for this, among others the fact that there are sharper conflicts and divisions concerning political questions in state administration than concerning the main goal of maximising profit in business life. This has probably entailed a greater degree of rigidity, and lack of 'daring', in state administration than in business life. However, it seems correct to add that the absorbent ability of state administration has—in our society—increased over the years. Absorption of 'progressive' goals (and a 'rounding of the edges' of goals) has become an important feature of government. This development of the state has gone so far that we may talk of 'an absorbent state' in some of the highly industrialised capitalist societies in Europe. In another context, I have discussed the further characteristics of 'the absorbent state'.[3] Here I am only emphasising the potential for suppressing protest which is contained in the tendency to 'take over' and 'fit in' goals which at the point of departure represent a strong protest, and how the state's character of being an absorbent mechanism contributes to the fact that silencing, which is very real indeed, remains silent.

Untraceable
In this chapter, I have taken as my point of departure silent silencing as it exists in the chain between background interests, executive organs and 'receivers' in the widest sense. The main point is that the interests which are the point of departure—the first link in the chain—do not have to delve into visible coercive arrangements or take any concrete coercive steps, because the later links in the chain largely simply act in accordance with the first ones. Thereby, no traceable silencing takes place, the real silencing which in fact occurs is hidden from both the participants themselves and from outside observers.

Furthermore, I have discussed two main types of 'problems' which may emerge in connection with such silent silencing. Firstly, errors or dangers may occur or develop which cause the third link in the chain, 'the people', to begin to think differently and more in the long term. Secondly, positive events or conditions may occur or develop which cause people to begin to think differently. That is to say, alternative goals may be set up and begin to become important in people's minds. Both types of conditions or events are 'problems' in the sense that if the circular relationship between background interests, executives and a 'public' disciplined to support those interests is to be maintained, a smaller or greater use of concrete force is easily called for.

---

[3] See my book *Law, Society, and Political Action*, Academic Press 1980, *Chapter 6*.

Demonstrable arrangements of coercion are, in our society, easier to criticise, more difficult to legitimise, and more productive in terms of protest in wider circles. Therefore it is—again in our society—important for the background interests to seek strategies which neutralise the two main types of problems, and which thereby maintain the hidden character of silencing. Above we have discussed a long series of such strategies, though it should be pointed out that the list is not exhaustive. Silence is maintained without concrete means of coercion being used; visible coercive methods are made unnecessary.

This does not mean that visible methods of coercion are never employed by representatives of powerful interests in our society. It does mean, however, that powerful interests in many situations and in many contexts in our society try as far as possible to avoid such methods, for the reasons I have given. As pointed out above: when the surface is clean and shiny in the sense that no external injunctions, and certainly no police or other 'noisy' methods, are brought into prominence, we do not see the kind of political silencing which in fact takes place. On this basis silencing is maintained while we all believe that we are free—and precisely *because* we all believe that we are free.

It is toward this real, deeply hidden and invisible coercion, that our political struggle should be directed. This does not imply that we should not struggle against the use of visible and demonstrable means of coercion in everyday life. We should only be prepared for silent silencing being in the background, and for the fact that the struggle against visible means of coercion in *everyday life* may become something of a struggle against shadows, because they—in everyday life—are not fundamental despite their visibility. The visible and demonstrable means of coercion are present, they are invoked when the crisis gets tough, and in the last instance we must therefore be prepared to struggle against them, but on the way we must also take up the struggle against silent silencing which is the silencing of the grey everyday.

THE BATTLE AGAINST SILENT SILENCING

The battle against silent silencing in everyday life may be fought in several ways. The main aim will be to *unmask* how silent silencing functions in the various chains in our lives. This is the first step in a (long) development toward political action. Let me mention two main roads to it.

In the first place, we may seek to generate—provoke—the use of visible and demonstrable means of coercion. If we manage this, our unmasking has paradoxically succeeded: we have managed to show that the issue in fact concerns silencing, and we have done so in a way which is threatening to the legitimacy of those who employ such means. However, it is far from always true that the means of coercion which are thereby employed, however threatening to legitimacy they may be, create the consciousness we want. When the means of coercion are 'provoked', their employment—mediated through our mass media, which sift and filter information—may 'hit back' and function as a still more conserving mechanism in 'public opinion'. The demonstration of the presence of silencing by provoking the use of visible and demonstrable means of coercion is therefore—if it is to be politically fruitful—an art which needs co-ordination, maximum concentration, detailed knowledge of how the various channels of communication function, and a considerable understanding of the needs of given population groups.

A large number of terrorist political actions (carried out for example by the Italian Red Brigades) in the third quarter of the 1900s in Europe obviously functioned far outside the range or reach of this art. They were extremely counter-productive and politically highly dangerous. Terrorist actions of this kind may be understood *inter alia* against the background of the massive silent silencing which actually rules us with an iron hand without the rule being comprehended, and without our managing to 'break through', but such actions are nevertheless politically reactionary in consequence. In addition they are, in my view, morally unacceptable. But other types of 'provocations', always non-violent in character, may under given circumstances be successful and acceptable—like when a prisoners' organization sends material on organizing to people in prisons, and the material is stopped by the prison censor, or when the same organization sends inquiries to prisoners asking them to contribute to a book, and the inquiries are stopped through the same censorship.[4] The Swedish socio-political journal *R* (signifying four socio-political organizations with the letter R in their names) has, through a number of cover stories and reports through the years, functioned brilliantly in this way; as has the well-known German 'provocateur' Günther Walraff. A decisive point is that no third party suffers from the result of the 'provocations'. But at the same time, it is decisive to 'co-ordinate' the various moves, so that the use of overt coercion is communicated in a way which in fact unmasks the system. In order for this to happen, it is important to have solid contacts in the media, and it is important not to 'exhaust' the method—the third time exposure of censorship in prison is set in motion, the event no longer functions as news.

This leads us to the second road: we have to be aware of the fact that the media may betray us because they are ruled by a market economy and by their own political premises. Therefore it is imperative to supplement actions of the above-mentioned kind with a broadly based unmasking activity in everyday life. Such direct description and analysis may take place in issue-oriented interest organizations, in political parties and in academic life. The unmasking of silent silencing through direct description of it across a broad range of fields might be one (though not the only necessary) basis for a common front. Silent silencing is, after all, common to all political organizations which are broadly on the 'Left' side. In isolation from each other, our various presentations become nothing but pinpricks which wither away when we are worn out. Together, we may work on a wider scale, and co-ordinate our activities.

This is one way in which to work in the time ahead—at least in the Norwegian and Scandinavian context. By this I do not mean that work of the kind which has been suggested here can or should stand alone. But it must be included, and be woven into the fabric of political initiatives. If it is not included, a highly significant aspect of the continual political silencing, and thereby of political rule, will pass us by.

---

[4]   These examples are taken from the political work of the Norwegian prisoners' organization KROM. Details may be found in my book *The Politics of Abolition*, Martin Robertson 1974.

3 Silencing Through Pulverisation

CHAPTER 3

Silencing Through Pulverisation

Oil extraction in the North Sea has, through the years, entailed the loss of many lives. When lives are lost, fundamental questions are often raised concerning the activity which is involved.

When fundamental questions are raised, conditions which were earlier seen as isolated from each other, are placed in relation to each other. As far as oil extraction is concerned, this implies that one sees the relationship between for example the profit motive and the lack of security measures at sea, the profit motive and the pace of extraction, etc.

And when *many* people perceive such a totality or context, the activity itself begins to be threatened.

Because people's perception of totality or context is dangerous to an activity like oil extraction, it becomes important for the representatives of the activity to *pulverise* the relationships which people begin to see. One of the most important ways in which to pulverise revealing relationships is to isolate the event which was the point of departure from the rest of the activity which the event is a part of. In other words, it becomes important, so to speak, to cut the event out of the fabric in which it exists. Such pulverisation of totality or context becomes more important the more extensive and sensational the event is. Under such circumstances, pulverisation becomes a significant means of bringing people back into line, that is, of silencing them anew.

ISOLATION TECHNIQUES

The catastrophic capsizing of the oil rig 'Alexander Kielland', proudly named after one of Norway's classical authors, in March 1980 in the North Sea, was just such an extensive and sensational event. Therefore, it was of maximum importance to the authorities, and to others who supported and carried through this—literally speaking—breakneck activity, *to isolate the event from the rest of the oil activity of which the event was an integrated part.* Such isolation of the event would ensure or at least increase the likelihood of continued silence and acquiescence among rank and file Norwegians.

If you manage to isolate the capsizing of a huge oil rig, and the loss of 123 human lives, from the oil extraction for which the rig was constructed and used, that must be said to be quite a feat. But to a very considerable extent, the political authorities and their allies in certain of the mass media managed precisely this feat during the first days following the catastrophe.

They managed this by the use of various *isolation techniques* in their comments on and discussions of the capsizing. When I employ the word 'technique' here, I presuppose that an element of consciousness and planning is present, but I wish to emphasise that the degree of such consciousness and planning may vary, and that other issues also have been prominent in the consciousness of the users in connection with some of the 'techniques'.

The isolation techniques discussed below are actually general, in the sense that they are used wherever it becomes important to pulverise a context in order to maintain an activity. We will therefore be exemplifying processes of a very general kind. I will describe and exemplify seven important and effective techniques of pulverisation or isolation. I do not undertake any quantitative content analysis, but concentrate instead on politically central statements in the press and other media.

To those who receive political messages via the mass media, the messages largely do not appear as 'isolation techniques'. Though they are techniques of domination, they therefore function as a hidden or unnoticed form of silencing.

Some of the techniques have also been discussed in *Chapter 2*. Here they are examined in the context of a major and terrifying event, which created shock waves throughout the Norwegian state machinery.[1]

The event is individualised
The first isolation technique which will be mentioned was also the first to be used during the sequence of events itself in the North Sea: the event was made into something unique, something incomparable, and something quite special, individual, and atypical. The implication of such a presentation is that the event is something from which far reaching conclusions concerning any change of course cannot be drawn—for that purpose, it is far too exceptional. The Norwegian government at the time was social-democratic, the Labour Party was in power, and a long editorial about the event in the main social-democratic newspaper *Arbeiderbladet* published 29 March 1980 gives several examples of this isolation technique.

'Tragedy in the North Sea', the paper headlined its editorial. Beyond doubt, the event was terrible; nevertheless the very headline itself to some extent gives the event the connotation of being something unusual, something you did not expect. (Because if you were continually anticipating a tragedy, you would not have initiated the activity in the first place.) The first sentences of the following text carry further implications that the event was something quite special: 'Prime Minister Odvar Nordli has characterised the almost unbelievable thing which now has happened in the North Sea as one of the greatest tragedies in recent Norwegian history. And in modern times it has in fact not happened that so many human lives have been lost in a single accident in our country'. And the editorial continued, in a similar vein, as follows: 'The accident on board "Alexander Kielland" is no regular oil accident as we are accustomed to think of.

---

[1] As of 2004: Several of the techniques of pulverisation discussed here may also be viewed as the authorities' attempts to deny the truth. See Stanley Cohen, *States of Denial: Knowing About Atrocities and Suffering*, Polity 2001. As I have said, my presumption is that the techniques are quite general. Therefore they are also likely to be present in connection with more recent catastrophic and strongly revealing events where important capital or state interests are involved. It would be interesting to see a similar analysis of such modern-day events as the Kursk tragedy in August 2000 (when a giant Russian nuclear submarine of the most advanced type suddenly and unexpectedly sank with a crew of 118 stranded aboard in the icy waters of the Barents Sea), or the Rocknes tragedy in January 2004 (when a large Norwegian cargo ship with a crew of 23, many of whom drowned, capsized in a matter of seconds about 100 metres from land, right outside the Norwegian city of Bergen). It would also be interesting to compare recent political events, such as the discovery in 2004 of the widespread use of torture, performed by the American occupation forces, in Iraq's prisons. The Bush administration appeared to use many of the techniques of pulverisation analysed in this chapter.

It concerns a catastrophe which no one could have believed would happen, almost as unthinkable, as if the City Hall of Oslo suddenly one day should collapse'. The idea of the absolutely exceptional, the unique and completely abnormal—and therefore, the non-generalisable—is very prominent.

It is interesting to note that an editorial in *Arbeiderbladet* used almost exactly the same form of presentation, and almost exactly the same words, in its introductory remarks concerning a fire on the Statfjord A platform in the winter of 1978. The reader may compare with the statements quoted from that editorial in *Chapter 2*. To repeat: the processes we are discussing are general.

The event is normalised

The second isolation technique is in a way the counterpart of the first: it consists of transforming the event into something usual rather than something unique, something repetitive rather than incomparable, something general and relatively typical rather than something special and atypical, something ordinary rather than out of the ordinary. But the following is very important if such 'normalisation' of an event is to become an effective technique of isolation: the event must be pulled out of its regular context and made normal and usual within another context, so as to isolate it from its original context. Concretely, this means that the 'Alexander Kielland' event in the North Sea had to be pulled out of its oil context and made into something relatively common and expected within another frame of reference.

This isolation technique was used very extensively during the first hours and days after the platform capsized. The director general of the Oil Directorate stated to the paper *Dagbladet* on March 28, when answering a question as to what consequences the accident might have for oil exploration: 'Here we are first of all confronted by a tragic accident which we must find the causes of before we can say anything about its consequences. But the accident is more like a ship's accident than a catastrophe tied to the oil activity'. The event was, in other words, normalised within a navigational context. The social-democratic newspaper *Nordlys*—a northern Norwegian paper extensively read in the areas where exploration for new oil fields had been initiated—stated in an editorial on March 31, *inter alia* that 'the North Sea accident is not the first one in the sector of energy supply. Through a number of years the coal mining accidents were the great tragic thing in this sector, and still coal mining accidents with many victims occur'. Here, then, the accident is normalised within a mining context. The head of the Norwegian national oil company Statoil's information service stated to the same paper that 'in magnitude the accident in the North Sea may compare with the greatest airplane catastrophes we have had, and obviously it may be said that risks are involved in all kinds of modern activities'. Here the event is normalised within the context of aviation, and in general terms simply within 'all kinds of modern activities'. And so on. In a commentary in the conservative *Aftenposten* on March 29, the issue was summarised as follows:

> A point which, however, is emphasised in Parliament circles and in informal talks with *Aftenposten*, is that the accident is not directly tied to the oil activity itself. The platform is a hotel rig, and drilling is not done on board. Therefore, the relationship with oil technology and drilling is not obvious. Comparisons with a hotel accident on

shore, the wreck of a ship with many passengers, or the risks involved in shipping
and fishing quite generally, are considered as much closer at hand.

And in a commentary in *Arbeiderbladet* on the same day, the issue was summed
up as follows: 'Rolf Hellem [social-democratic member of Parliament at the time]
thinks that the hotel rig at the Edda-field does not have anything to do with
active drilling. If comparisons are to be made, they must in his opinion be made
with shipwrecks, hotel fires, and similar accidents'.

Again, it is striking to see how almost exactly the same words and
expressions were used concerning the above-mentioned fire on the Statfjord A
platform in February 1978. The event then was normalised by comparisons with
accidents in general in dangerous work performed under difficult conditions, as
well as with the mining accidents. Again, it was not 'a typical "oil accident"'. The
reader is invited to make a comparison with those statements quoted *Chapter 2*.

The event is split up
The third isolation technique is the technique which isolates the event from its
context by splitting or dividing the event into its more or less free-flowing and
unrelated bits and pieces. In its editorial on March 29 about the 'Alexander
Kielland' tragedy, *Arbeiderbladet* stated:

> given the accident, it seems as if the rescue service has functioned as presupposed
> and according to plan. But also here there is a need for review in order to find still
> better solutions. Among other things, this time there seems to have been present a
> weakness in communication during the important first phase, a weakness which it
> should be possible to safeguard against. In addition, once more we saw in practice
> that the evacuation possibilities from the installations are too poor when an accident
> actually occurs. Also in this respect new efforts must be made to find better methods.

The event is reduced to particulars in connection with rescue routines and
security rules, whereby the totality is easily lost. Note again, how the same
newspaper used almost the same words in connection with the Statfjord A fire in
February 1978—the reader is once more referred to the preceding chapter.

I am not denying the actual importance of such questions. The point is that
by being pulverised, the context fades and recedes into the background in favour
of the unrelated questions of detail which are in focus. And all the time it is taken
for granted that the 'accident' has happened, and in a sense had to happen.

The event is placed in the future
When you are trying to form a total or overall understanding of an event, it is
important to know about the past, present and future of that event. And it
becomes correspondingly important—to those who wish to prevent someone
from forming a total perspective—to isolate the past, the present and the future
of the event from each other.

The fourth isolation technique which will be mentioned here, is therefore the
technique which places the event, or at least central aspects of the event, in a
more or less distant future which has not yet been reached.

Could this particular isolation technique be used in connection with
something as blatant and factual—and so clearly pictured for all and everyone on

television—as the catastrophe in the North Sea? It could in fact be used, and was in fact used massively. Under the main headline 'Oil and Energy Minister Bjartmar Gjerde: "The rescue action is the only important thing now"', the then minister of oil and energy *inter alia* made the following statement to *Arbeiderbladet* on March 19: 'This is not the right time to discuss possible consequences of the catastrophe in the North Sea'. And the paper commented on the statement in the following words: 'In his reply, the minister included political consequences as well as the question of whether the situation would have any bearing on the question of exploration for oil north of the 62nd parallel when summer comes'. Two weeks before the catastrophe, the Norwegian Parliament had decided to open the oil fields north of the symbolic 62nd parallel during the summer of 1980. Very central questions tied to the event were in other words put off to a distant and vague future.

The same tendency was noticeable among representatives of the largest political parties—representatives of the Conservatives and the Labour Party together with the Liberals. *Aftenposten* quoted representatives of the Conservatives and the Labour Party on March 19 in the following way:

Willoch restricts himself to stating that he finds it meaningless to enter any debate now concerning possible consequences of such a catastrophe. Neither are people in Labour Party circles willing to discuss consequences or draw conclusions before the casual background has been clarified.

The same view ran through several editorial comments during the days immediately following the event, for example as follows in *Aftenposten* on March 29:

This is not the time for making bombastic statements concerning the consequences which the North Sea catastrophe should have. So far we know little about the causes, and before these are clarified by the public investigating committee which now has been appointed, we are unable to draw any definite conclusions.

In addition, the same editorial provides one of many examples of how the various isolation techniques were combined during the days following the event. Immediately after the quote given above, the editorial continued with 'normalisation' of the event, in these words:

At a press conference in the Government Building yesterday noon, the Prime Minister was asked whether the oil activity is worth the price which we have had to pay in this case. It is a legitimate question, which of course may also be raised in many other contexts where activities are carried out at the risk of life and health.

The last sentence might very well have continued: '—activities which we think are worth the price'.

To repeat, by in this way placing important aspects and issues tied to the event in the future, these aspects and issues are put off for a more or less indefinite period. When the time finally comes, people generally have put a distance between themselves and those who lost their lives.

The event is isolated in the present

The fifth isolation technique is intimately connected with the fourth one: at the same time as important aspects and issues tied to the event are put into a distant and vague future, maximum emphasis is placed on the human or humanitarian aspects of the case *in the present*. Serious top politicians are photographed boarding special planes which are to bring them to the accident area, and statements such as the following—by the minister of Oil and Energy, Bjartmar Gjerde, to *Arbeiderbladet* on March 29—are very typical: 'What we now have to concentrate on is the rescue action in the Ekofisk area. All possible methods must be used to make that as effective as possible.' Of course, the rescue action was important. The point here is that central politicians created further isolation between present and future aspects of the event by combining the placement of them in the future with a maximum emphasis on certain humanitarian aspects in the present. Individual politicians who, during this early phase, overstepped the mark by suggesting the possibility that the event had to have consequences, for example for the issue of exploration north of the 62nd parallel, were in certain media regarded more or less as desecrators of corpses.

The event is relegated to the past

The sixth isolation technique is that which isolates the event from its context by relegating it more or less to an outdated past. Again: was this possible in connection with an event such as the one in the North Sea? It was made possible by emphasising that the concrete subject of the incident—in this case the oil rig 'Alexander Kielland'—was outdated and simply not of the kind which in a few weeks would be in use north of the 62nd parallel. For example, on April 1 *Arbeiderbladet* could explain—after an interview with the chairman of the Labour Organization for oil workers, in which the chairman said that the weather and working conditions further north during the summer months were not much worse than those of the North Sea:

> In addition, [further north] the plan is to use an entirely different rig, ... a platform of Norwegian design—Aker's H-3. This is a platform which is constructed in an entirely different way. It consists of two hulls which are bound together by four crosswise connections. The Aker Group has constructed it in this way for security reasons. Therefore, the experiences from the ... catastrophe cannot simply be transferred to Aker's type of rig.

This was considered important despite the fact that the catastrophe on the 'Alexander Kielland' only days before had been characterised by experts as 'unbelievable' and 'unexplainable' (*Arbeiderbladet*, March 29: 'This could not happen'). Why Aker's H-3 platform clearly would be more secure, and the difference decisive, remained unclear. (At the same time the newspaper gave yet another example of the many combinations of isolation techniques: it continued its presentation by saying that such a transfer of experiences from the 'Alexander Kielland' type to Aker's type of rig 'would be the same as transferring experiences from one type of airplane to another after an accident. The DC-10s were stopped after the accidents last year, but the Jumbos continued to fly'.)

The Northern Norwegian paper *Nordlys* was even more outspoken on March 29, under the five-column headline 'The Commander of the Oil Rig which is going

to Northern Norway in the Summer: "A Similar Accident Cannot Happen Here"'.
The article contained the text:

> While the wrecked platform is built in France according to a special system which to-day in a way is more or less outdated, the rigs 'Treasure Seeker' and 'Ross Rig', which are going to Northern Norway, are built according to an entirely different principle in Singapore and Norway respectively.

This was stated under the subheading 'Entirely Different Platforms', and the commander of 'Treasure Seeker' who was interviewed, continued by saying *inter alia* that 'our platforms can under no circumstances capsize ... It can simply not happen'. It is only the words 'in a way' and 'more or less' in connection with the word 'outdated' which do not make the 'Alexander Kielland' rig suddenly appear as *dangerously old fashioned*—again in spite of the fact that around the same time that capsizing was also characterised as 'unbelievable' and 'unexplainable', something which 'could not happen'. The commander ended his story to the paper by stating (despite the fact that the investigating committee which had been appointed had not even begun its work) that he could not 'with the best will in the world automatically transfer the accident on board the "Alexander Kielland" to our own rig, or to other comparable rigs. On board our rig we continue our work.'

In brief: by relegating the event to an outmoded past, the event is made untransferable to other parts of oil extraction.

The event is elevated to history

The seventh—and, in this chapter, the last—isolating technique which I wish to mention is the one which pulls the event out of its concrete context—in this case oil production—by elevating and including it in a much more general historical context, 'the history of man'. *Nordlys* put it in the following words in its editorial on March 31:

> The forces of nature are violent, and despite security measures and preventive measures against accidents, a 100 per cent guarantee cannot be given, here or any other place. Accidents have, unfortunately, followed man through his history and will follow us also in the future.

Here then, past, present, and future are seen in relation to each other, but, it should be noted, on an entirely different and general historical level. *Arbeiderbladet* used still more flowery words as early as two days after the event, on March 29, again in an editorial:

> The exploration for oil at sea is the work of pioneers. In all such work we will from time to time suffer setbacks. It is hardest when human lives are at stake. If we were to give up every time a setback of this kind occurred, we would not have come far on the road toward the society we wish to live in. Also after a tragedy we must collect ourselves again, and continue.

In the light of history, man becomes a minute creature.

*

To repeat: through the individualisation of the event, the normalisation of it in other contexts, the splintering of it, the placement of it in a protected future, the isolation of it in the present, the relegation of it to the past, and the elevation of it to History with a capital H, the context within which an event takes place is pulverised. In this particular case, the context is oil exploration at sea, under the particular security and work conditions, and with the particular possible consequences, which this implies.

As I have suggested already, the techniques which have been mentioned are general: with variations and concrete adjustments we also find them in other contexts where appalling human events throw a new and glaring light on a field of activity where those responsible have given assurances that everything is in order.

Precisely the same techniques were employed when conditions at Reitgjerdet Hospital were beginning to be exposed. Reitgjerdet was a Norwegian psychiatric hospital for patients characterised as psychotic and dangerous. It took patients— or better, prisoners—from other mental hospitals and from the prisons. Over a number of years the institution was severely criticised for the brutal and generally scandalous treatment of its inmates. When the brutality of the institution was finally revealed to the general public, attempts were made to individualise the whole situation (the conditions at this particular hospital were presumably unique in the Norwegian system of mental hospitals); attempts were at the same time made to normalise it (the institution was defended through references to similar or related conditions elsewhere, inside and outside the system of mental hospitals); to splinter it in its minute details (the relevance of various measures of physical coercion used in the hospital was defended through particular case histories); and so on. A majority, if not all, of the techniques discussed in this essay were employed in connection with the Reitgjerdet scandal.

As in connection with so many other 'scandals' of a similar kind. In sum: the understanding of context, of structure, of pattern, is dangerous. To those in power.

FROM 'ALEXANDER KIELLAND' TO 'HENRIK IBSEN' – ISOLATION TECHNIQUES AGAIN

Note that a concluding and near-catastrophic event was waiting in the wake of the 'Alexander Kielland' disaster. One afternoon, ten days after the catastrophe, radio and television reported the sensation that 'Alexander Kielland's' sister rig, the hotel rig 'Henrik Ibsen', had heeled over by more than 20 degrees at the large Philips base in Tananger. The direct cause of the heeling was the fact that a number of 'manholes' had been open during an inspection of the rig by Veritas (the body responsible for the classification and certification of Norwegian ships), a fact which had not been known to the commander. The rig, which was floating very high during the inspection, was lowered and water began to pour in. The heeling was stopped only by the fact that the shaft of the rig hit the bottom of the sea.

Interestingly, the use of the isolation techniques, and the pulverisation of context, to a large extent also continued after this event.

   This was the case in other places, among editorials for example in politically central newspapers such as *Aftenposten* and, in particular, the social-democratic papers *Arbeiderbladet* and *Nordlys*. In *Nordlys*—the paper closest to the coming exploration north of the 62nd parallel—the tendency was especially marked, as some details from its editorial on April 8 1980, the first working day after Easter, clearly indicate. This newspaper *normalised* the latest event by emphasising that such a thing

> has of course also happened to other seagoing vessels. In Northern Norway we have, during the last decade, had several tragic and unexplainable accidents with modern seagoing fishing vessels. 'Lack of stability' has been suggested as an explanation of some of these wrecks, in which many human lives have been lost.

At the same time, the 'Ibsen' as well as the 'Kielland' events were discussed in terms of 'this platform construction', so that the *unique* was emphasised: the paper was 'in full agreement with the Labour Organization which has taken the stand that no oil workers should live on the new hotel platform 'Henrik Ibsen' before all aspects of the 'Alexander Kielland' accident have been clarified'. Other types of platforms, of which there are several, totalling a large number of rigs, were in other words not included; on the contrary and by implication they were clearly excluded. And the 'Kielland' as well as the 'Ibsen' events were made part of the *past*: 'as far as we know, the platforms to be used in the activity outside Northern Norway are not of the same kind ...' The headline on the first page of the paper was, typically, 'Human Error is the Cause'. How many 'accidents' are to take place before the various aspects of oil exploration at sea are to be seen in relation to each other, and the fundamental questions of existence, pace, and expansion of the oil activity itself are really to be posed?

POSTSCRIPT

This chapter was originally written in Norwegian during the first two weeks following the 'Alexander Kielland' accident. It was printed within two more weeks, in April 1980, as a political attempt to influence public understanding of the dangers involved in the oil exploration in the stormy Norwegian waters.

   After publication in Norwegian, the various isolation techniques discussed above had time to work. For the benefit of English-speaking readers, the ensuing sequence of events will be briefly outlined.

   The main political issue in the oil sector in Norway around the time of the capsizing of 'Alexander Kielland' was the question of whether oil exploration north of the 62nd parallel should be commenced. There was already in Norway strong resistance against opening the northern fields. In the first place, public opinion polls before the catastrophe showed that there was a clear majority of Norwegian people (especially in Northern Norway) against exploration in the far North. Secondly, people in the fishing communities which would be affected had for a long time been strongly against the opening of the areas in the North. Some of the best fishing banks had been selected for exploration, and the habits of the fish and the activities of the fishing vessels would be directly and profoundly affected. Thirdly, important groups of experts had for a long time warned against opening the areas in the North. Considerations of security, environment, and occupational structure had been emphasised. In sum, Norwegian resistance against exploration for oil in the far North somewhat resembled the resistance in other countries against the use of atomic energy.

In spite of all of this, a majority vote in the Norwegian Parliament (with the Labour Party and the Conservatives in the majority against three small centre parties and the Socialist People's Party) had, on March 13, advocated commencement in the North in the spring of 1980. The exploration activity was to be limited to the summer months.

Then came the 'Alexander Kielland' catastrophe on March 27. Despite the catastrophe, exploration activities in the Northern fields commenced almost exactly as planned. On 30 April 1980 the cabinet ministers responsible gave an account to Parliament of the political effects of the catastrophe, and on May 6, six weeks after the accident, a new majority vote in Parliament renewed the permission to start exploration in the North in the spring of 1980.

The isolation phase

One may ask, how this was possible? How was it possible for the Norwegian government, after the 'Alexander Kielland' catastrophe, to make oil activity in the far North become a reality only a few weeks later? Why was drilling for oil in the far North *at least not significantly delayed*; how could it start up almost on the day of the original plan—with flags and banners?

A very important part of the answer seems to lie in the extensive use of the isolation techniques which were discussed above. Their use, which pulverised the context of the event and reduced substantially the political significance of the event as far as oil production goes, indeed silenced those who otherwise would have protested against expanded exploration. Put differently, the isolation techniques were highly significant in making expanded exploration politically possible despite a catastrophe of such magnitude.

Furthermore, the extensive use of isolation techniques was followed up by three further and concluding political phases which, that spring, so to speak crowned the achievement of making expanded exploration possible.

The reconstruction phase

Following *the isolation phase*, a second phase could be termed *the reconstruction phase*. Against the pulverising background of the isolation phase, the Government or its members and its like-minded allies could proceed to the construction of a new story of the event and of the role of the Government itself.

The Ministry of Community and Work Affairs sent a letter to the Oil Directorate, the Navigation Directorate, and the Norwegian body Veritas, in which the ministry asked the agencies to consider whether, after the 'Alexander Kielland' wreckage, there 'has already come to light circumstances which from a professional point of view make it necessary to introduce changes in the oil activity?' The letter to the three agencies was presented to the public as a result of the Government's general evaluation of the situation, and the prime minister was solemn when he appeared on television that night. The Government would not wait for the clarification of these important issues until the investigating committee had concluded its work: the investigating committee would take months, and the Government would certainly not wait that long. The Government would demand replies to its letter very quickly—by the end of the month. And when reviewing the replies, the Government would not only consider the question of exploration in the North, but the oil activity as a whole. Such was the urgency of the case.

The whole presentation gave a highly responsible impression, and inspired the greatest confidence—how could one suspect such a government of simply wishing to continue the expansive nature of existing oil policy? What remained unstated, was the fact that reports 'by the end of the month' in any case would be *necessary if the Government wished to commence oil exploration in the far North as planned*. If it wished to follow schedule in crossing the 62nd parallel, it would be impossible to wait for the investigating committee: to repeat, that committee would take months. The reports from the three agencies were published after less than two weeks, and solemnly presented on the television news. It appeared that the reports emphasised certain marginal changes in resources and routines, but they did not provide any basis for a more fundamental change of course. With these three reports, the foundation in oil policy of adhering to the status quo was in reality laid. The fact that the 'reports' from the Oil Directorate and the Navigation Directorate actually consisted of two thin and hurried letters, of four to five pages each, was never mentioned.

The politisation phase
The following, third phase could be termed *the politisation phase*. On the basis of the 'reports', and certain additional materials, the Government was now in a position to formulate its policy anew: exploration as planned north of the 62nd parallel. The formulation took place publicly in Parliament on April 30, in the form of oral presentations by the Minister of Community and Work Affairs and the Minister of Oil and Energy. Because the great catastrophe was so recent, it was important to give the conclusions a slightly preliminary, and thereby responsible, character. The oil minister pointed to the investigating committee: 'In view of the brief time which has passed since the accident', he emphasised, 'and the fact that the report of the investigating committee is not yet available, it is today too early to draw final conclusions concerning possible consequences for the oil activity'. A 'broader discussion' would be 'natural' after the appearance of the report. The balancing was delicate, but the essential question could be answered: it was 'the opinion of the Government that there is no reason to maintain the division which in fact has existed in our waters along the 62nd parallel'.

The legitimation phase
Taken together, the three first phases constituted a comprehensive preparatory justification or legitimation of exploration north of the 62nd parallel. Nevertheless, it is possible to discern a fourth, concluding phase, *a legitimation phase,* in which particular external and highly symbolic forms of legitimation of the exploration plans were intensively employed.

When the 62nd parallel was crossed on May 12 by the first Norwegian rig, 'Treasure Seeker', this was celebrated by spirited news interviews, and on May 14 *Harstad Tidende,* the local newspaper in the little Northern Norwegian town where 'Treasure Seeker' was to have its final checks before starting its actual programme, could tell its readers on its front page: 'When "Treasure Seeker" comes to Harstad: "Open rig" for the first time in history'. People were invited to come on board to look. The public relations officer of the shipping company which owned the platform, had this to say to the newspaper: 'When it comes to oil rigs, you usually hear of Americans and soft-ice. Therefore we hope to have the soft-ice machine on "Treasure Seeker" working at its maximum on Monday May 19.' This was the day when people were to come on board. A large group of local businessmen were given lunch on board, some 40 journalists were given a special tour, and 720 local inhabitants were shown around—and generously treated to soft-ice. At the time I was a visiting scholar at Norway's northernmost university, the University of Tromsø, and a group of us from the university were also given a special tour. In a quarter-page advertisement on the front page of the social-democratic Tromsø paper *Nordlys*, the shipyard wished the platform 'Welcome to Harstad!' and 'The best luck with its task in the North'. In short, flags, banners, tours, lunches and soft-ice were indeed used.

In brief: the important and splintering isolation phase, in which the numerous techniques of isolation spelled out in this essay were employed, was followed up by a reconstruction phase, a politisation phase, and a legitimation phase. Together, the four phases made possible what many had viewed as utterly unthinkable after 'Alexander Kielland': exploration north of the 62nd parallel exactly as planned. Its commencement silenced the public debate, and a resistance which had lasted for years, and which threatened to become a real danger to the Norwegian state and capitalist oil policy, was more or less terminated. It is a crucial point that its commencement was finally triggered not by the use of physical means of coercion, but by the most suave of methods—methods of silent silencing.

4   System and Silencing

CHAPTER 4

System and Silencing

Some years ago, the question of the 'system' of bureaucratic organizations—their internal structure and functioning—occupied a central place in the understanding of conservation and change in social conditions. In particular, public institutions—state systems in the widest sense—were analysed this way: the question of state organizations as 'systems' had a central position in connection with sub-areas of society as well as in connection with social life more generally. The internal mechanisms of the 'system' were analysed as restraining and furthering of change—in more detail, of change within structural frameworks as well as transformation of structure. Furthermore, the mechanisms of the 'system' were analysed as abstracted from, or independent of, the social context within which the 'system' functioned and was an expression of.[1]

In recent years, this type of 'system analysis', and the emphasis on the more or less inbuilt tendencies of the 'system' to function in given ways, has to a considerable extent been replaced by analysis of class and interests. 'Systems', organizations and their inherent 'systemic' features have been less prominent in such analyses, while the question of background interests, especially class interests and their significance for stability and change in social structures, has grown correspondingly in importance.[2]

In connection with the choice between these approaches to the issues of stability and change, however, a combination of the two viewpoints easily suggests itself. In more detail, it is easy to think in terms of bureaucratic state organizations, with 'system features', as intervening links—that is, links between background class antagonisms and interests—on the one hand and the 'result', in the form of stability or change in and of social structure, on the other hand. This is to say that features of the state organization, the 'system', function as a 'filter' between class antagonisms and interest constellations on their way toward the 'result'. To be sure, class antagonisms and interest constellations will frequently be directly represented in the organizations: a part of the class struggle itself is in other words sluiced into the organizations and takes place there regardless of internal system features. This is the case whether we are speaking of the class struggles of the early and middle 1900s or the more complex and splintered class structures of our own time. But more or less general mechanisms, built into the system of organizations, nevertheless tend to filter these antagonisms and constellations, so that the result is not given simply against the background of class conflicts or external power relations. For example, it seems that the potential power of the working class in the early and middle 1900s was neutralised partly through the functioning of the 'systems'. In exactly this way

---

[1] An example of such an analysis may be found in my book *The Politics of Abolition*, Martin Robertson 1974. Here the concept of 'system' is used frequently and 'system forces' are analysed as independent of the interest and class contexts which the 'system' operates within and is an expression of.

[2] Of course, there are nuances in the picture.

the state becomes a comprehensive apparatus with the function of maintaining the stability—or, alternatively, achieving the change, mainly on its own terms— of society.

Such a combination of views has appeared in some sociological works; among others, in some works on the sociology of law.[3] It might be said that the combination of views implies an integration of points of view from both classical Marxist and classical 'Weberian' theoretical angles. The classical Marxist angle emphasises class antagonisms and the interest constellations as governing societal stability and development. The classical Weberian approach emphasises the mechanisms of the 'system', especially of the 'bureaucracy', which are assumed to function as they do abstracted from the contexts of class and interests in which the system exists. The combination of these views assigns weight to both sides, and assumes that the result is determined by this two-sided emphasis.

In today's political as well as sociological debate, it is probably important to emphasise precisely this combination. A pure 'system analysis' might lead to erroneous political conclusions, for example to the conclusion that organizations—especially state organizations—are organized independently of the environment, from which it in turn follows that organizations may be moved in the direction wanted simply by 'putting out of action' opponents inside the organizations. A pure 'class analysis'—'class' again taken in its classical or more modern sense—leads to correspondingly erroneous conclusions by a failure to perceive the formative or governing mechanisms within the organizations— precisely the mechanisms of the system. For example, one might risk overlooking the very strongly absorbent effect which bureaucracy has on political struggles which could otherwise have been won in 'open' societal terrain.

SYSTEM MECHANISMS

Notwithstanding the importance of both sides of the issue, in my opinion the *formative influence of system mechanisms* is today overlooked in the analysis. The sociology of complex organizations has in a strange way faded or even disappeared from the sociological agenda, at least in Norway.[4] To bring the sociology of organizations back onto the agenda is a pressing task. Below I shall therefore concentrate on system mechanisms, in order to illustrate what is lost if such mechanisms are not taken into consideration.

By 'system mechanisms' I mean here the built-in features of organizations which are activated and which begin to function under certain conditions. I wish

---

[3] See, for example, Håkon Lorentzen; *Systemkrav og aktørtilpasning—en analyse av politiets arbeid i vegtransportsektoren* (System Demands and Actor Adjustment—An Analysis of Police Work in the Road Transport Sector), Masters Thesis 1977 for an attempt at a theoretical and empirical analysis of this type. As of 2004, see also Ole Hammerslev, *Danish Judges in the Twentieth Century. A Socio-legal Study*, Jurist- og Økonomforbundets Forlag 2003.

[4] Classical works like Amitai Etzioni's *A Comparative Analysis of Complex Organizations*, The Free Press 1961, and Peter M. Blau and W. Richard Scott's *Formal Organizations. A Comparative Approach*, Chandler Publishing 1962 have been little followed up in Norway. In the early part of the 1960s Norwegian sociology was greatly preoccupied with the sociology of organizations, and important works appeared on the prison, the mental hospital, the industrial plant and the social structure of the ship. Later on, the emphasis largely disappeared. This still holds as of 2004.

to deal with five such system mechanisms, which have the function of quieting opposition to decisions made in the higher ranks of the system (and the decisions forced on the higher ranks of the system from outside), and generally of quieting opposition to the mode of operation of the system. This implies that we are discussing mechanisms which have a silencing effect on political opinions and political actions. The fact that political silencing in this way is built into the organizations, and that through them the political authorities do not have to lift a finger to quieten opposition, is frequently overlooked in political analysis and debate.

Refusal to participate and marginal benefits
I shall first of all mention a mechanism which implies that those in potential opposition come to accept the procedures of a given system and to participate in them, rather than opposing them and pulling out on grounds of principle.

It will often be the case that clients—in a narrow or wide sense—*lose marginal benefits through their refusal to participate in particular subsystems or activities within organizations.* For example: a social worker in a prison refuses, on grounds of principle, to participate in decisions concerning the punishments of prisoners, and is willing to leave her job if she has so to choose. She is immediately met with the counter-argument, from the other employees, that if she does not participate and thereby leaves her job, this will only increase further the chances of the punishments being imposed. In actual fact the likelihood of the social worker influencing these decisions is very small, because she and others like her are always in a minority, but it becomes even smaller if she does not participate.

Established authority systems frequently have such marginal benefits built-in for clients. This holds not only for prisons, but for the police and other formal organizations of control, and for state administrations generally. The marginal benefits do not change the situation of the client in anything but small details (and often not even that, but there may be a *chance* of small changes), but details may be important in the critical or concrete situation. The building-in of such benefits places the clients' spokespeople (whether they speak for limited groups of clients, such as prisoners, or as political spokespersons for larger population groups) in a situation of conflict: refusal to participate, which may be desirable on grounds of principle (to liberate oneself from strings which might prevent articulated political opposition, to raise the consciousness of others about the weakness and erroneous orientations of the system), entails a reduction of the clients' actual or potential marginal benefits. Through this mechanism, refusal to participate on grounds of principle is placed in conflict with the interests, albeit marginal, of the clients.

This mechanism of control does not only function in relation to the question of full or total withdrawal from an established subsystem or practice. It also penetrates further into the system, into the inner layers of the onion, as it were. On all—or at least on many—levels of the organization you are confronted by the same conflict: the conflict between not participating in decisions which on grounds of principle you would prefer not to participate in, and the possibility of loss, through refusal to participate, of marginal benefits for clients. This way you are easily 'absorbed into' the system in question, and into participation on a series of levels in the system which by their very nature, are dubious. You become 'a part of' the system.

Participation and marginal benefits
Secondly, it will often be the case that clients—again interpreted in a narrow or a wide sense—*lose marginal benefits from their opposition within the system once entry and permanent participation has been decided*. For example: in some circumstances social workers who work with vulnerable young people frequently wish to protest against the use of physical violence by the police, which they know young people are often exposed to. The social workers know, however, that if issues of police behaviour and police violence are taken up, this may in fact result in the increased use of violence by the police against young people, and that the young people themselves for this reason are wary of such issues being taken up.

This way, not only is refusal to participate grounded in principle prevented by the built-in marginal benefits which participation may give to the clients. In addition, once participation has been decided opposition is silenced for the same reason. You do not so easily perceive the latter point when you stand at the entrance of a given subsystem or level within the system. You therefore often think that participation, which may be problematic and in conflict with your principles, may be offset against your chance to oppose once you are inside. Once you are inside, the guns may be taken out and fired. However the possibility of loss of further marginal benefits may prevent this as well.

In this connection it is important to realise—and to emphasise, even if it has been said already—that the acquisition of marginal benefits on the part of clients *does not alter their more general and basic position in a total social structure*. This is precisely what characterises the *marginal* benefits. By this I do not mean to say that the marginal benefits may not be worth the fight: to repeat, small changes and improvements may be important in critical or concrete situations. The point is that due to them, and due to the system's control over them and the system's possibility to purchase silence with them, it frequently follows as a fact that opposition *is* silenced.

Isolation when decisions are made
Thirdly, representatives of client interests in a system—the concept of 'client' all the time taken in a narrow or wide sense—often remain isolated, or at least in a minority, in all or most of the arenas *where actual decisions concerning the clients' interests are made*. In other words, even if interests may have mass support outside the administrative organization in question, they will tend to have minimal support where the actual decisions are to be made.

Put differently: In the decision-making bodies of the organization, you are—even if at the outset you have significant or even massive support from the grass roots—to a large extent a lonely spokesperson for client interests. The decision-making bodies are not constructed so that the grass roots or ground levels are directly represented in proportion to their real quantitative strength. Rather, they are organized corporatively, which is to say that a series of different interests are represented around the table. Such interest representation is regarded as 'democratic' since all or most of the parties may participate and are able to have their say. But it easily leads interests which have broad grass roots support into minority positions, because the other representatives around the table have different interests. The struggle to acquire alliances in corporative decision-making systems is often hard, involving many compromises and uncertainties, and it is certainly far from always successful. I would emphasise that this also holds true even if other interests do not conflict with one's own in the actual case at hand: the possibility that the interests may conflict later, in other cases or over other issues, often make the other interest representatives reserved when it comes to giving support.

In the more or less lonely role of spokesperson, it is again a priority to quieten your opposition. To get your views through, or at least to get them through as far as possible, it frequently seems tactically wise to 'lie low'. To be sure, by keeping a high profile you may alternatively create political publicity around the demands, and have a consciousness-raising function in circles around the decision-making body. But this presupposes that the people in the environment are 'present'—either directly as participants or indirectly through the reach of the mass media etc.—to receive the message. Frequently this is not the case. There are several reasons for this, and some of these also have to do with the structure of 'the system': important decisions are made in particular bodies inside organizations which are placed in such a position that the environment simply cannot be there, or people are not motivated to be there.[5] Decisions are made more or less in secret. An example would be the delegation of the actual decisions to 'preparatory' bodies: for example to committees which 'prepare' the issues for further handling in the final decision-making bodies, where they pass through without debate.

In other words, we are confronted by a quite clear example of the inner structure of a system as producing ideas—here the idea that it will be profitable to lie low. The low profile which we frequently find—in the most varied contexts—among spokespeople for interests which are actually controversial, is probably precisely tied to this: the structural position of the spokesperson in question is such that silence, or at least a type of thinking which is strongly watered down, presents itself as expedient and wise. This low profile may be found over a broad spectrum of issues, from the distant corners where decisions in socio-political affairs are made to the central questions in production and work life.

Side-tracking—into details, abandonment and caution

Above we have mentioned first how the existence of marginal benefits makes you participate in a system which you might have wished to avoid on grounds of principle, next how the possibility of attaining the marginal benefits in question silences your opposition after participation, and finally how the construction and structural position of decision-making bodies leads you into a more or less isolated position within them, a fact which additionally silences your opposition.

---

[5] I emphasise that the reasons also have to do with the 'environment' itself: lack of organization outside the system, the political profiles of the mass media, which filter news about what is taking place inside the system, the interest of the mass media in selling rather than in covering politically important decisions, etc., play their role. We are here at a typical 'intersection' between external and internal conditions—see the introduction to this chapter. To repeat, I see it as my task here to emphasise internal conditions.

We shall now add a fourth factor, which is *how opposition, in addition to being silenced in the ways we have suggested, is channelled into side tracks*, that is, into issues and questions which are more or less unrelated to the political stance of the opposition. This fourth factor in turn has many aspects. I will illustrate three of them.

Firstly, channelling into side tracks occurs in bureaucratic organizations when general or comprehensive political questions are split into greater or smaller details, whereby the struggle is *transferred to questions of detail* rather than the general or main issue. The sociology professor, for example, who tries to strengthen Marxist inspired traditions in a law faculty, remains—within the decision-making bodies—mainly preoccupied by winning the issue of whether three particular pages in a Marxist inspired textbook rather than three pages in another textbook are to be part of the curriculum.

Secondly, side-tracking occurs through *the abandonment of the political question* which was the starting point for the benefit of quite different and politically much less important questions. These less important questions are pressed upon you by participants in the system who have mastered and dominated the formulation of issues currently in the system. The sociology professor who tries to strengthen Marxist inspired traditions in his law faculty is forced to read thick piles of documents and prepare himself for dealing with the issue of whether administrative law should be part of the first or the third year of studies for law students. Because the question may have a certain significance in a long-term perspective, he must engage himself in it, 'to be on the safe side'.

Finally, side-tracking occurs through the abandonment of the general political view which was the starting point in favour of *a much more cautious view*, again because the more cautious view is pressed upon you by the participants in the system who master and dominate the formulation of issues. The sociology professor who tries to strengthen Marxist inspired traditions in his law faculty thus becomes primarily preoccupied with securing, in the general administrative law curriculum, a briefly presented state analysis which is at least somewhat more sociological in orientation than the rest of the administrative law curriculum.

All these examples illustrate how an opposition is also silenced by being channelled into issues and questions which are distant from the political point of departure.

Interhuman relationships: initiation, shift of perspective, shared responsibility
Initial participation due to possible marginal benefits; silenced opposition in order to attain some of the marginal benefits; isolation in corporative structures where decisions are made; and side-tracking. At this point, a fifth important silencing link may be added: You are additionally silenced, and muted in your opposition, through the interhuman relationships which you enter into after initial participation and the first rounds of silencing have become matters of fact. Close interhuman relationships are established simply through participation in the organization. These have certain important psychological consequences which are highly silencing. I will divide them into three.

Firstly, an *initiation into internal secrets* takes place through participation in decision-making bodies. The initiation is necessary if you are to be able to participate in decision-making, or to prepare (as a 'case-worker') for decisions to be made. The internal secrets may be official or unofficial secrets, and explicit or implicit professional secrecy may be tied to them. Often the unofficially defined secrets, and the implicit professional secrecy, are the most important; in most cases they cover a much broader range than the officially defined secrets with an attached explicit pledge of secrecy. Through initiation into secrets you become tied to the people around you, and to the organization or department which has initiated you into them. This way you are subdued or hesitant in your attempts to 'go outside' with information, you become cautious when criticising the organization on the outside, and you acquire a community or fellowship of secrecy with those who originally were your opponents inside the organization.

This occurs if the initiation is tied to a formal initiation ritual, such as a more or less closely planned security clearance (either performed through an evaluation of you by the organization or by investigations undertaken by specialists) about which you do not get detailed information, but which you know takes place. Perhaps precisely because you do not get detailed knowledge about it, the clearance functions as a ritual to you. But the same also occurs even if no formal ritual is involved—it occurs every time a piece of information is conveyed to you with a solemn or informal reminder that 'this is internal', or simply with the unspoken understanding that this is 'between us'. Such individual and informal initiations are 'stored': as you learn and know continually more, 'inside', about and in the organization, acquiescence becomes all the more natural.

A second and related way in which interhuman relations in organizations silence you, is by a *shifting of perspective* which is produced through participation in decision-making bodies. Questions which arise, and decisions which consequently are made, are increasingly, as you participate closely alongside others, seen from within rather than from the clients' external viewpoint. From within you 'see' all of the difficulties tied to 'cutting through' and making a client-oriented decision. The difficulties are partly of a bureaucratic character: if you 'cut through', this will have further effects on decisions and decision-making bodies elsewhere in the system. Also the difficulties partly have to do with your relationships with other inside participants: from within you see that other participants may be mobilised against the decision you wish to make, participants on whom you have become more or less dependent by your being initiated into their secrets and through their initiation into your secrets. On both grounds, the perspective is easily formed that it will be very difficult to make given decisions even if the decisions look fair and simple from the outside. Let me emphasise that the shifting of perspective has a structural basis: you could 'cut through' both the bureaucratic obstacles and the inside criticism were it not for the fact that bureaucratic obstacles as well as criticism from fellow participants actually become important to you and your own affairs in the organization. *The shifting of perspectives itself is, then, to a large extent if not exclusively a question of membership in and dependence on a structure.* In other words, the shifting of perspectives is based on a type of corruption, and not on pure perception, due to skewed information.

A third way in which interhuman relations in the organization silence you, is that you begin to share *responsibility* through participation in collective decisions.

You have entered the system because of the marginal benefits etc., you have begun to participate in the decisions of the system, and you are therefore 'part of' the decisions which are made by your colleagues *and* yourself. You have already been driven into issues and questions which are only pale shadows of your basic standpoint. Even if you have taken a minority stand in these pale shadows of issues, you are nevertheless 'defiled' and made responsible together with others through the participation itself. You become still more responsible if you let the view of the majority go through without even minority votes or statements, which you frequently do as a part of an internal long-term tactical plan—you really wish to muster opposition when a tactically good case comes along. This sharing of responsibility quiets your opposition to the decisions and the system: you have participated in the decisions, and by that token you have to a greater or lesser extent vouched for them. Shared responsibility also makes you more vulnerable when facing criticism for the decisions from the outside, which in turn makes you defend the decisions—at least your own participation in them.

Endpoints: Roles for former oppositionists
Through initiation, the shifting of perspective, and shared responsibility, you are driven continually further into the system. At worst you finally end up in one of the many roles that exist for former oppositionists in bureaucratic organizations.

One of these roles is that of the *radical alibi*: you maintain a certain harmless opposition which functions so that the system itself appears as tolerant and open. Another is the role of *ambiguous bridge-builder*: you maintain a certain contact with the opposition on the outside and give the impression of building a bridge between it and the system, but you do so in such a way that the viewpoints and demands of the opposition are effectively trimmed. A third is the role of *professional technician*: in the organization, you define yourself as the executor of a delimited field or profession which presumably has no contact with the question of your degree of opposition to the interests which the system promotes. A fourth—and perhaps the last in some people's development—is the role of *resigned defector*: you maintain certain ideals from your past or your youth, but you believe it is unrealistic to adhere to the ideals in practical work, and you therefore give them up in the work situation itself. A fifth—and probably the last in other people's development—is the role of *active defector*: you no longer maintain your old ideals, but you clearly leave them behind and dissociate yourself from your earlier thinking and earlier companions. You become a system worker.

Combinations of these roles are also possible. This way we may say that a 'moral career' is formed for many of those who enter the system.[6] Put differently: the various system mechanisms which have been discussed here may constitute steps in a moral developmental process on the part of the individual who enters. Not everyone goes through the same steps, and sometimes the steps certainly appear in a different order, but the following full order may undoubtedly be found. The marginal benefits first lead you to participate in the system and its sub-systems. Then the possibility itself of attaining the marginal benefits begins to mute your opposition as a participant. You are additionally subdued through the structure of the decision-making bodies: you are frequently isolated, or at

---

[6] The concept of a 'moral career' is taken from Erving Goffman, *Asylums*, Doubleday 1961.

least in the minority, a fact which makes you quiet down for tactical reasons. Furthermore, the opposition which is left in you is channelled into issues and questions which are distanced from your political point of departure. When this point has been reached, you begin to enter interhuman relationships which are additionally silencing: through initiation into secrets, shifting of perspective and finally shared responsibility, you are pushed so far into the system that you easily end up in one of the roles modelled precisely for and by former oppositionists. Possibly, you pass through the various roles in a sequence, from functioning as a radical alibi via the roles of ambiguous bridge-builder and professional technician to the roles of resigned or active defector. But, to repeat, several of the roles may also be played simultaneously.

OPPOSITION IS POSSIBLE

Through examples I have so far in this essay emphasised the significance of 'system mechanisms' for political silencing. I repeat that external conditions, outside the organizational systems, are not thereby seen as unimportant. The final and total silencing effect probably results precisely from a combination of external and internal conditions. For example, the silencing which takes place within and through the general school system constitutes a foundation which makes the later internal system mechanisms function in a fully silencing way: The mechanisms are allowed to function without any significant opposition.

The next question is this: what would happen if opposition was in fact established against the silencing mechanisms? Would they become neutralised? A general point of view may be outlined: imperative mechanisms or conditions are precisely as imperative as men and women assume and accept them to be. This does not mean that every opposition necessarily will be successful. It does not mean that an opposition may not 'run its head against the wall' and fail. But it does mean that successful opposition is possible in principle. If a sufficient number of people stand together in opposition, if necessary far outside the particular system in question, the imperative framework may be transcended. More precisely, solidarity in opposition, which is possible in principle, is the basic condition for the abolition of coercion. It is precisely by splitting and isolating opponents from each other that the silencing mechanisms, grounded as they are in the preparatory silencing of the education system and the total socialisation process, may function so well. Thus it is by attempting to counteract the splintering character of the mechanisms that silencing may be subdued and by voicing alternative opinions, criticism and protest may be fostered. Let me add that academic sociology has been tragically unable or unwilling to help people develop strategies for such 'counter action'. Academic sociology has largely said: only what is, is possible.

Another way of putting it is to say that the mechanisms which we have discussed are not inevitable in their effects; in principle they may be abolished, and in practice they may at least be limited.

Consciousness and selectivity

The first point in this process is *that of becoming conscious of the silencing mechanisms*. Analysis of, and continual reflection around, the mechanisms may contribute to this. It is my hope that this chapter may have such a function.

The second point in the process is *that of becoming conscious of the significance of being selective* with regard to systems, in case you choose to enter one. I personally have more or less continually warned social workers and others against entering the prison system. I have been of the opinion that the marginal benefits are so small, and the mechanisms of silencing so strong in this system that there is great danger that you will be completely subjugated without the clients receiving anything in return for it. I should think that the same holds for certain other parts of the state's apparatus for physical violence. The situation is somewhat less clear with regard to other state systems, and in practice it cannot be expected that a total boycott of all of these will gain a hearing. This is especially so in times of widespread unemployment. Neither is such a boycott politically desirable. But to repeat, it is important to be selective, or at least as selective as possible. Systems vary with regard to the strength of existing opposition both inside and outside.

Organizing—inside and outside; intra-professional and inter-professional

The third point—which is an extension of the second—is *that of organizing with others who also are in opposition to one's membership system, or to other parallel systems*. Organizing of this kind is the crucial point. It may take place *inside* the system, as a direct attempt to neutralise the silencing tendencies of the system. But it may also take place *outside* the system. Firstly, outside organizing may be an anchorage point for the individual, in which the individual may find support for his or her oppositional viewpoints, discuss instances of his or her possible bowing to the system, and receive support for the view that it is possible to stand up straight again. Secondly, outside organizing may help the individual find channels for political work—jointly with others—outside the system where he or she has a work connection. Silencing forces are often less overwhelming for the individual outside his or her work system. In such political work it will often be possible to use knowledge and experience from one's work system, and it will contribute to the maintenance of one's political profile inside the work system.

I regard political organizing *outside* the system as an absolutely necessary condition if the silencing mechanisms are not to get an upper hand in one's work inside the system. This holds whether you concretely channel your political engagement in issues outside or inside the system. The question is, then, how political organizing outside the system is to be implemented in more concrete ways. Two possible forms will be mentioned here. On the one hand, one may organize *intra-professionally*—as lawyers, as sociologists, as social workers. There are examples of such organizing—partly as trade unions, partly as more oppositional alternatives to the traditional trade unions (like the Norwegian critical lawyers' organization among jurists). On the other hand, one may organize *inter-professionally*—around broader or narrower issues or issue areas which may engage across professions, and which may simultaneously engage the client groups in question (the Norwegian prisoners' organization KROM constitutes an example of such organizing).

Personally, I believe more in inter-professional organizations which at the same time include non-professionals than in intra-professional organizations. In the first place, no society generates professions in a narrow sense which systematically work against the society itself; there is only room for such professions during the starting phase of the profession, or as long as the profession does not have very significant societal functions.[7] Secondly, restricted professional groupings easily become primarily oriented toward the needs of the profession, which may be limited compared to the broader political issues. Thirdly, such groupings will very likely be narrow in method or approach, a fact which will be a political limitation because the political issues require a broad range of approaches. The first of these three problems is probably the most important one.

This does not mean that it may not be important, at given points in time, to form professionally delimited organizations. The foundation of the Norwegian critical lawyers' organization in 1974 was probably very important and correct in the view of the situation of radical lawyers at that time. Neither does it mean that such organizations should be quickly transformed or abolished. It may very well be correct to maintain, for example, the critical lawyers' organization in its present form for a long time (transformations are probably dubious during politically hardened times such as those we have now). But for reasons I have indicated, and especially because the professions as narrow professions are so strongly determined by underlying societal needs, I would think that it is important, over time, to seek to channel organizational work in the inter-professional direction. Organizing of this kind provides an opportunity to take up political issues in a broader way, it gives the individual professional an opportunity to see and meet others who have problems which are comparable to his or her own, and—not least—as alluded to above it provides an opportunity for organized contact over and above the professions, that is, with the 'users'.[8]

The essential and crucial political organizing which I have suggested here, is not simple from the point of view of implementation. Such a 'simple' fact as the state of *the labour market* is sufficient to create great difficulties: when it is difficult to find a job, or when it is easy to be laid off, the organizing easily crumbles. The question of finding or keeping a job takes priority over the maintenance of organized opposition. The situation in the labour market most certainly also penetrates the silencing system mechanisms themselves: when the individual has difficulties in finding a job, or when he or she is easily laid off, the mechanisms are more easily left in operation without opposition.

It is, therefore, important to make the decision to be conscious of such complicating circumstances, and jointly to strengthen the organized opposition particularly in such difficult times.

---

[7] For a more detailed presentation of this point, see *Chapter 5*.

[8] An example: the fact that the Norwegian prisoners' organization KROM has *combined* professional competence with the insight of clients, thus combining theory with practice, has probably been one of its assets. It is probably this combination which at least in phases has made the organization appear threatening in the eyes of the authorities of the criminal control system: it has been impossible to place the organization in one or the other 'box'.

5   Sociology:
A Silenced Profession

CHAPTER 5

Sociology: A Silenced Profession

A basic thesis in this chapter is that sociology as a discipline, and the sociological profession, are undergoing a fundamental change of character in the direction of greater emphasis on *applied research activity*. More precisely, there is a development in the direction of *applied research activity financed and in a wide sense initiated by the state or by state related bodies.*[1] The implicit or explicit expectation from state agencies is that the research results will be useful to them. Knowledge, useful to the state, about the 'effects' of social arrangements is hailed. Frequently, the researchers themselves apply for the grants, but they do so on the basis of frameworks drawn up by the state.

A further basic view in the chapter will be that the general applied profile which sociology is gradually taking on is of significance far outside the ranks of sociologists alone. In particular, I wish to discuss three main consequences of this development: firstly, an attitude and activity emphasising societal symptom reduction rather than causal analyses; secondly, an ideologically legitimating effect for the state which in turn follows; and thirdly, a political silencing which this development also entails for social scientists in a broad sense. These three consequences will be discussed in this order.

Let me emphasise that these are not the only consequences of the development mentioned above. Let me also emphasise that symptom orientation, state legitimisation, and the silencing of social scientists are not without their nuances and exceptions. There do exist examples of important critical contributions within state financed and state initiated research activity. And good examples may be found of researchers who stand up against the three processes and refuse to yield. However, it is my view that the consequences are present as *significant tendencies*, and that they probably will be all the more noticeable in the years to come.

One could summarise it as follows: signs of oppositional, critical sociology still exist, but as a main tendency critical sociology is in the process of being silenced, in particular due to its state-applied character and development.

If we do not very soon make this into a central question for debate, we will drift into the applied—silencing and legitimating—main profile almost without noticing it. If, however, it is made into a central question for debate, and seen as a question of great significance to each of us, we may be able to curb the development at least to some extent. More about this later.

In order to throw light on the main theme which I have outlined here, I shall try to show the situation of sociologists in today's Norwegian society in a broad historical perspective. The sociology profession is not the first profession to have

---

[1] In this chapter, the concept of 'state' is taken in a wide sense, including not only state institutions specifically (for example ministries), but also municipal administration and other public institutions at least partly financed by the Government, Parliament or the municipalities. To a great extent the concept simply refers to 'state institutions' in the specific sense. In other places the context will, I think, clarify the meaning.

entered an applied main profile. Great professions have gone before us and done exactly the same, even if the concrete conditions and forms have been somewhat different. We may, therefore, learn from history.

More concretely, I shall review some features of the development of the professions of law and economics. Their fate in Norwegian society may be seen as related to two great main phases in the development of capitalist society. I shall try to show precisely how these professions became great and powerful against the background of the tasks which they 'applied themselves to' in each main phase. Against this background I subsequently arrive at the sociologists, and their position as applied researchers. I see the growth and development of sociologists in their turn as having gone through two further phases: a first phase which created a basis for their quantitative growth, and a next phase which is now creating the basis for their transformation to a politically speaking very silent and acquiescent applied research activity.

Taken together, then, we will be discussing four main phases in the development of Norwegian society. This way I hope to convey how the fate of the sociologists is a part of a much larger picture, having to do with the relationship of the professions to the society in which they are created and function. The sociologists, particularly in their last applied variant, constitute the last link in a long chain of development.

THE INITIAL PHASE—AND THE LAWYERS

The first main phase of the development of capitalist society which I shall deal with[2] may be called *the initial phase*. I am referring to the very breakthrough of capitalism, which in Norway and several other European countries took place through the 1800s and into the 1900s. This was an extended phase which obviously saw comprehensive crises in the capitalist economy, but in which the very development of the capitalist economy as such was more important than the planned and systematic control of its crises. The crises, it was assumed according to classical liberal theory, would even out and be solved through the market mechanism—'the hidden hand'.

Which academic profession was most important in the extended initial phase of capitalist society? In the Norwegian context, the lawyers had their period of greatness in the 1800s, during the first development and building of the capitalist economy and social formation.

Law and confidence
Vilhelm Aubert and associates have shown how the number of lawyers and ministers was about even in Norway in 1815—right after the opening of the first Norwegian university (in 1811, as part of the liberation in 1814 from 400 years of Danish rule)—with 400 ministers and 329 lawyers. At the same time, there were

---

[2]   The phases of the development of the capitalist social formation which I emphasise here do not constitute the only possible classification, and—if one were to write the history of Norway—it is obviously a highly simplified one. I suggest the classification because it throws light on the development of the academic professions and the general question which this chapter deals with.

160 medical doctors.[3] But the lawyers were at the beginning of a great expansion. As early as 1844 we in Norway had 450 ministers, 800 lawyers and 259 medical doctors. Among these three professions the lawyers were now clearly in the lead. And they increased the lead throughout the century—in 1864 the figures were 567, 1250 and 354 respectively; in 1895 they were 700, 2000 and 910—and, into the 1900s—in 1905 they were 720, 2400 and 1210; in 1930 731, 3200 and 1775. Elsewhere Aubert has commented on the figures as follows:[4]

> If it could be said that the University of Copenhagen [which was the university also for Norwegians in the 1700s] was a school of ministers in the 1700s, it may be said that the Royal Fredrik's [the first Norwegian university, opened in 1811] had, way into the 1900s, as its foremost pedagogical task that of being a school of lawyers.

What may be said about the causes of, and/or the functions of, the lawyers' pronounced growth and domination in the 1800s and far into the 1900s? Aubert has commented on the development as follows:[5]

> In a peasant society the population will have confidence in relatives, neighbors, and certain authority figures. But there are few social bonds which may create a basis for confidence beyond this narrow circle. From this, a number of difficulties follow when new economic activity is to be initiated. Credit, trade, loyal tax payment, new work contracts, the establishment of banks and shareholding companies, presuppose that confidence may be created between persons who have not had a chance to test each others' responsibility through years of personal contact ... I present the hypothesis that *the development of a large legal profession in Norway contributed to creating a basis for confidence at several points in society where this was a critical condition.* [author's italics]

I believe there is much to be said for the hypothesis which is launched here. The breakthrough and the first development of capitalism did in fact create new economic relations beyond the 'narrow circle', whereby the question of confidence between economic actors who were strangers to each other became great and serious. It should be noted that the issue here is confidence *within* a growing upper class, not the development of confidence across social classes.[6] In sum: during the initial phase of the development of the capitalist economy and social formation, the question of confidence within an upper class constituted a main problem, and the lawyers could contribute to the solution of that problem. In terms of jurisprudence, the development of a whole new civil law—based *inter alia* on principles from Roman law—was particularly important.

The applied task of the lawyers
In other words, the *applied task* of the lawyers during this important phase could be said to be that of creating the above-mentioned basis for confidence within a new economic system. In slightly more detail: during the period 1814-40, when Norway had to build its new state following the break with Danish rule, the

---

[3] See Vilhelm Aubert *et.al.*, 'Akademikere i norsk samfunnsstruktur 1800-1950' (Academic Professions in Norwegian Social Structure 1800-1950), *Tidsskrift for samfunnsforskning* 1960.
[4] Vilhelm Aubert, *Rettens sosiale funksjon* (The Social Function of the Law), Universitetsforlaget 1976, pp. 256-257.
[5] Aubert *op. cit.*, pp. 257-258, my translation.
[6] See Aubert *op.cit.*, p. 258.

lawyers acquired a monopoly position in public administration.[7] But as we have indicated, the number of lawyers also continued its explosive increase after this period, paralleling clearly the actual breakthrough and development of industrialism in Norway. The applied tasks were not given to them in accordance with any general super-plan, but developed through an interaction between the needs of the new and growing upper class and the lawyers themselves: the lawyers became the hired helps of the new upper class. Thereby they constituted the first great profession to become the servants of powerful interests in Norwegian society.

THE PRIMARY CRISIS PHASE—AND THE ECONOMISTS

The second phase in the development of the capitalist society which I wish to emphasise may be called the *primary crisis phase*. The period before World War II increasingly saw symptoms of crisis in the heart of the capitalist economy— symptoms of economic crisis which culminated with the crash in 1929, with the economic problems of the 1930s and for that matter with World War II. Again, the following must be forcefully emphasised: obviously, rudimentary capitalism also saw economic crises before this time. Earlier, however, it could be said that the crises would be solved by the further development of capitalism itself, by capitalism as a full-grown system. Now—from the 1920s and on—this conception could no longer be maintained so easily. Capitalism had become a full-grown system, and had been in operation as a system for a long time in many places, but the crisis came *despite this*; the crisis was, as it were, 'paradoxical' in the light of current liberal theory, and therefore threatening in a new way which demanded new action.[8] Simultaneously, the crisis came during a time of strong development on the part of the new revolutionary organizations of the working class, with their background in the Russian Revolution of 1917. Altogether, a particularly strong demand for action developed in relation to the mounting crisis.

The lawyers—and jurisprudence—could not be as useful during the crises which our part of the world witnessed in the 1920s and 1930s. Now, the issue was no longer first and foremost the development of confidence and integration within an upper class—even if the lawyers certainly still had (and have) this function and still were (and are) important[9]—but rather the control of a critical

---

[7] Per Lægreid and Johan P. Olsen, *Byråkrati og beslutninger* (Bureaucracy and Decisions), Universitetsforlaget 1978, pp. 33-34.

[8] It may be said that objectively speaking, the crisis of the 1920s and the 1930s was not 'paradoxical, but, quite to the contrary, in keeping with the developmental logic of capitalism. What is at issue here, however, is the actor's subjective conception. The concept of 'crisis', which is difficult to define, is used here about 'situations in which established systems, in important sectors in society, no longer fill their function' (Ted Hanisch, *Hele folket i arbeid* (Labor for All the People), Pax 1977, p. 10). But something else must be added: 'Furthermore, the concept must be tied to the political legitimacy of the regime in office. If one is to talk about crisis, the failure of the functioning of established systems must be so serious that this legitimacy is being threatened' (ibid.).

[9] As of 2004, the Norwegian Lawyers' Association had just under 14,000 members holding the advanced degree (cand. jur) in law. The association represented about 85 per cent of those trained in law in the country. Over 30 per cent of the members were advocates. Norwegian lawyers today

development of the economy. And precisely during this period, another profession became crucially important in the arena of the Norwegian professions: *the economists.*

Keynes comes to Norway
The Norwegian sociologist Terje Rød Larsen has given us an important picture of the development of this profession (economists) for the very period which we are discussing here.[10] The training of economists in Norway was originally an activity which took place within the Law Faculty. There the study of economics was introduced as a brief so-called 'national economics examination' in 1905. The advanced degree in economics as we know it today was introduced, still within the Law Faculty, as late as in 1934—precisely at the peak of the primary crisis phase.

The British economist and lord, John Maynard Keynes (1883-1946), was a towering figure in the background—in Norway as in so many other countries. He had contacts in Norway: in 1938 he received an honorary doctorate at the University of Oslo. His ideas about an expansive economic policy fell on fertile soil, ready for such a message. Terje Rød Larsen shows how the new profession developed at the University of Oslo before World War II—under the leadership of Professor Ragnar Frisch, a Keynesian economist and later Nobel laureate—and how its further development took place during the World War II occupation. The profession continued developing in the secluded milieu of professional economists in occupied Oslo, in the political milieu of London (the exiled Norwegian government in London was strongly influenced by contact with Keynesian economics in England) and in other places (among others, Rød Larsen points out, in a German concentration camp outside Oslo, where a university fellow and later professor of economics organized 'seminars' in economics with the future top politicians of the Norwegian Labour Party).

In terms of figures, the profession of economics which was now growing, could not of course measure up to that of the lawyers. In 1945, the first post-war year, the number of economists receiving degrees at the University of Oslo was 18. This increased to 52 in 1950, after which it decreased to 40 in 1955 and 22 in 1965. Then a new climb began: to 77 in 1970 and 89 in 1973.[11] By 1970 there were 930 occupationally active economists in Norway.[12]

(especially those who work in the large law firms) have important functions in private and semi-private business, partly on a global level, where they are vital in developing creative contracts for large corporations engaged in transnational business. In other words, their applied service function for large-scale and small-scale business, their creation of 'a basis for confidence beyond [the] narrow circle' is still pronounced. See Knut Papendorf, *Advokatens århundre? Globaliseringen og dens følger for advokatmarkedet* (The Century of the Advocate? Globalisation and its Consequences for the Advocates' Market), Report No. 47 from the Norwegian 'Power and Democracy Project', 2002.

[10] Terje Rød Larsen, *Hjerte og hjerne. Om den norske sosialøkonomiske profesjon* (Heart and Brain. On the Norwegian Economic Profession), Institute for Sociology of Law, Oslo, mimeographed 1976.

[11] The figures have been supplied by Terje Rød Larsen.

[12] See Tor Kobberstad, *Arbeidsmuligheter for kandidater med juridisk og samfunnsvitenskapelig utdanning* (Labor Possibilities for Candidates with Legal or Social Scientific Training), The Norwegian Council for Science and the Humanities, 1975, p. 16.
   As of 2004: In terms of numbers, the greatest expansion in numbers of economists trained at the universities took place during the Keynesian post-war years covered above. As of 1999, there were about 1,800 trained economists in Norway (with an income of over 100,000 crowns). About half of

Better answers

But the profession mastered a theory—a Keynesian theory of economic planning—which was far better suited to the new problems than was any legal theory, and, as we know, during the years following the War the profession quickly moved into a number of central positions in Norwegian state administration and high-level politics. After World War II the study of economics was also, symbolically, taken out of the Law Faculty and placed in the new Social Science Faculty.

It is my supposition that the profession of economists and economic theory was developed, and developed out of law, precisely from the 1930s on because they provided better answers to the problems of the time than the law did. The content and theory of the profession was, as I have indicated, to a large extent imported from abroad, especially from England. But there too the new types of problems existed at exactly the same time, and the content of the profession and the theory would hardly have taken such a hold in Norway if the new critical problems had not been there as receiving soil. The march forward of the economists becomes, it may be added, a part of the march of the Norwegian Labour Party, and of this party's takeover and development of the state apparatus. In brief: during the primary crisis phase in our capitalist society, the economic profession began to equal, and perhaps to surpass, the lawyers—if not in actual figures, then in theoretical and political importance. The period of greatness for the lawyers and jurisprudence was the initial phase, when the foundation of confidence in the new production form was laid.

THE SECONDARY CRISIS PHASE—THE SOCIAL SCIENTISTS AND THE SOCIAL WORKERS

The third phase in the development of the capitalist society which I wish to look at may be referred to as its *secondary crisis phase*.

The second 'paradox'

The years following World War II witnessed a long period of even economic growth. At the same time, most of this long post-war period also saw an increasing critical development (in correspondence with the definition of 'crisis' given in note 8 above) over a broad socio-political spectrum: rising registered crime rates, increasing alcohol-use and drug-use, increasing frequencies of illness of various kinds, increasing use of social security benefits and similar signs of social exclusion, etc.[13] Again, this does not mean that comparable social

---

them were in the public sector, a little less than half in the private sector (five per cent in research). Source: Anders Ekeland and Thor Egil Braadland, *STEP Arbeidsnotat, Notat utarbeidet etter oppdrag fra Statskonsult* (STEP Working Paper, prepared for Statskonsult) Dec. 1999, www.statskonsult.no/it/itskatt/aekeland . Other types of education, in commerce and business administration (*siviløkonomer*), take place at various colleges.

[13] With regard to the official crime rates for the period, see Thomas Mathiesen, *Kriminalitet, straff og samfunn* (Crime, Punishment, and Society), Aschehoug 1978; with regard to alcohol use, see the same author, *Løsgjengerkrigen* (The Vagrancy War), Norsk Sosionomforbund 1975, p.41; with regard to drug- and alcohol use, see Olav Irgens Jensen and Mons G. Rud, *Bruk av stoffer, alkohol og tobakk blant gutter og jenter i Oslo 1968-1976* (The Use of Drugs, Alcohol, and Tobacco among Boys and Girls in Oslo 1968-1976), Universitetsforlaget 1977; with regard to rates of sick-leave, see Rolf

phenomena did not exist during earlier phases of development of the capitalist society. A broad spectrum of these problems could for example be found during the 1800s. The point here is that the spectrum of social crisis problems during the post-war years could not so easily be interpreted in terms of regular economic poverty and destitution, an explanation which could well be given for the social crises during the 1800s. Rather, and to repeat, the development of problems now took place in a particularly long, strong and even *period of growth* in the life of capitalism—in Norway with an increased standard of living for very large groups in the population. Thus, the development of problems was again 'paradoxical' compared to what one should expect (and, in addition, partly concealed by the general economic growth, which prevented a public and political definition of it as a full scale 'crisis'), and thereby threatening in a new way. Reference to the built-in potential for development of capitalism again constituted an insufficient basis for comfort; on the contrary, capitalism developed as 'positively' as could be expected, but the whole spectrum of problems continued to grow.[14]

In relation to the secondary crisis of the post war-years, neither lawyers nor economists could be very useful. The development of confidence within an upper class was obviously no longer the point, and—during the 1960s and the beginning of the 1970s—neither was the control of the economy. Rather, what were in demand were professions which presumably could do something with the signs of *social* crisis.

The medical doctors

First, of course, came the medical doctors. Above, we followed the quantitative development of ministers, lawyers and doctors up to 1930. In terms of figures, the period 1930-40 constituted a turning point for the medical doctors: in 1940 the number of ministers was about the same as it was before, 760, and the lawyers had increased by about 1,000 to 4,260, but now the doctors too had really begun to climb, with about 700 more, thus totalling 2,500. And in 1950—at the beginning of the post-war period which we are discussing here—the doctors, and not the lawyers, made the greatest leap: while lawyers climbed to only 4,800 (or by 13 per cent over the decade, base 1940), the doctors climbed all the way to 3,754 (or by 50 per cent over the decade, base 1940). The ministers were still hopelessly behind, totalling 828 (with a 9 per cent increase, base 1940). All the way from 1815 to 1940, the gap in absolute numbers between lawyers and medical doctors had been increasing. 1950 was a turning point, the gap began to close. By 1960, the race between lawyers and doctors was continuing and the gap continued to decrease, with 5,200 lawyers (an 8 per cent climb over a decade,

---

Hanoa, 'Utviklingen av sykefravær—sosiale og sosialmedisinske årsaker og konsekvenser' (The Development of Sick Leave—the Social and the Socio-Medical Causes and Consequences), *Sosial Trygd* 1977; with regard to the use of social security benefits, see Knut Brofoss and Ståle Eskeland, *Rett til arbeid?* (The Right to Work?), Institute for Sociology of Law, Oslo, mimeographed 1975, especially p. 174, and Knut Halvorsen, *Arbeid eller trygd?* (Work or Social Security?), Pax Forlag 1977. Some of the data for the period are summarised in English in Thomas Mathiesen, *Law, Society and Political Action*, Academic Press 1980, chapter V.

[14] As of 2004: The trends outlined here have largely continued, but in a more hesitant way for several of the types of behaviour mentioned. The registered crime rate has recently been going down.

base 1950) and 4,350 doctors (a 16 per cent climb over the decade, base 1950). In 1970 the doctors were definitely in the lead: that year there were 5,188 lawyers and 5,685 doctors in the country.[15]

The expansion in the numbers of doctors may, however, just as well be seen as an expansion of a type of service to the population in general, a type of service which also serves the capitalist economy and which a social-democratic regime (as was more or less continuously in office during the post-war decades) is obliged to develop. But simultaneously new professions developed, with a stronger and clearer orientation toward the signs of the social crises and their background.

Enter the social scientists and the social workers

From the universities came the social scientists, *inter alia* the sociologists and the political scientists, and from various colleges came the social workers. The ideological basis for the development of these professions again came from abroad—for example from the United States—and the ideas were developed there during similar periods of social crises.[16] In addition, it was now—and neither before nor later—that the ideas really took hold in Norway. Interestingly, university training in sociology began—as did training in economics—*inter alia* with lectures in the Law Faculty in Oslo before World War II, and when the Institute of Sociology at the University of Oslo was established in the Historical-Philosophical Faculty around 1950, it shared offices with the Institute for Criminology and Criminal Law in the Law Faculty. Later the social sciences made their complete break-away: the Social Science Faculty was established, and training in the social sciences developed particularly from the mid-1960s and into the 1970s. By the end of 1976, about 200 students had received advanced degrees in sociology, and about 320 had received similar degrees in political science.[17] In the first part of the 1970s, a practice-oriented social science line (the so-called 'cand. sociol./cand. polit.' degree) was particularly on the increase, especially among political scientists.[18] The first social work college in Norway was

---

[15] As of 1 October 1999, the last year for which I have figures, there were around 16,000 medical doctors in Norway, and approximately the same number of lawyers—see note 9.

[16] For example, the great and well-known 'Chicago School' in American sociology between the world wars—which trained a number of the most well-known American sociologists—was developed with the spectrum of 'social problems' in metropolitan Chicago as point of departure. The development of American social work clearly had a similar background. The great influence on sociology of Talcott Parsons' grand theory of society, culture and personality during the post-war years, especially his notion of 'social systems', can actually be viewed in a similar light: the theory constituted a great attempt to reconstruct and conserve Western societies in the face of deep social problems following the shattering international experiences during World War II.

[17] I emphasise that these are approximate figures. They result from a summation of sociologists/ political scientists 'living in Norway' at the end of 1970 (found in Anne Marie Ivås, *Yrkesundersøkelse for psykologer, statsvitere, sosiologer og etnografer i 1970* (An Occupational Study of Psychologists, Political Scientists, Sociologists, and Ethnographers in 1970), Norwegian Social Science Research Council 1973, p. 32 and p. 35) and 'Candidates receiving final degrees at Norwegian and foreign universities' 1971/76 (found in *Norske studentar og kandidatar* (Norwegian Students and Candidates), Norwegian Social Science Research Council 1977, p.2 8).

[18] As of 1 October 2002, there were about 1,800 people with advanced degrees in sociology, and around 2,650 with advanced degrees in political science. 'Political science' is here broadly defined, also comprising *inter alia* advanced degrees in public administration and organization, public policy and administration and social planning. Close to 28 per cent, between one-quarter and one-

established as early as 1920, but the next college did not follow until 1950, and the others, in various parts of the country, came in 1962, 1966 and 1967—precisely during the development of the secondary, social crisis phase of the capitalist society. By June 1975, a total of 2,380 social workers had received their degrees from the social work colleges. In 1974 and 1975 the figures were 225 and 250 respectively. Later on, social work education became integrated in the many general colleges which were established.[19]

Together with the social scientists trained at the universities, the social workers constituted a *new professional grouping specifically oriented toward the various types of social problems under capitalism.* The social scientists probably provided a kind of theoretical superstructure, with a monopoly on knowledge of a theoretical kind, while the social workers were a kind of infantry, primarily trained for client work. Contact between the two sub-groups was not much, but the infantry read a good deal of what the university trained social scientists wrote—just as the practising lawyers read the legal dogmatics of the university jurists.[20] But both sub-groups—this is my thesis here—were given conditions for growth, development and jobs, against the background of the massive problems which 'paradoxically' followed in the wake of the best growth period of capitalism. I am not asserting that these massive social problems constituted a sufficient condition for the development of the new professional category, but I am supposing that they constituted a necessary condition, and that they promoted the growth of the category in a very significant way. The new professions suited the emphasis which the social-democratic state little by little had to place on finding solutions to the above-mentioned 'human' problems, problems which followed from the structural development of capitalism.[21]

One point should be emphasised: it is important to realise that the social scientists/social workers—like the economists before and alongside them—did not contribute significantly to solving the 'causal questions' behind the problems. At best, what these professions primarily did was to alleviate some of the symptoms. However, what they were successful in achieving was to *strengthen the legitimacy of the state and of a society which was highly productive of serious problems.* It gives an impression of rationality, planning, and sound judgment when professional executives with such training and prestige as the economists, or in such great numbers as the social scientists and social workers taken together, are employed to address the problems.[22]

---

third, of political scientists belonged to one of these categories (information from the Norwegian Census Bureau).

[19] As of 1 October 1999 there were about 6,700 social workers, trained at the various colleges, in Norway.

[20] By this I do not mean to say that the parallel between the social scientists/ social workers and the lawyers is complete. For example, the lawyers do constitute one single profession—the practising lawyers have all been trained at the universities—while the social scientists and the social workers must be seen as two professions within a grouping: social workers in Norway are not trained at the universities.

[21] Concerning the relationship between the structural development of industry and the production of social problems, see Knut Halvorsen, *Arbeid eller trygd?* (Work or Social Security?), Pax Forlag 1977.

[22] As far as the social workers go, 'the state' is taken in a wide sense, more as 'public administration'. About 70 per cent of Norwegian social workers have jobs in various parts of municipal administration (figure as of 2004). See note 1.

These twin functions—the alleviation of symptoms and the increase of state legitimacy—are two central functions of the problem-oriented professions.[23]

*

In this way we see that the three first phases of the development of our society have been followed by a development of three corresponding professions or professional groups. The professions have in a pronounced way had an applied, service relationship to those responsible for solving the critical problems which the phases have produced. The applied task of the lawyers was that of creating a new basis for confidence, the task of the economists was that of creating a less chaotic economy, and the applied task of the sociologists—thus far—was that of softening certain agonising contemporary social problems as well as providing legitimacy to the state. And the development increasingly moved in the direction of applied research activity, research activity which was financed and in a wide sense initiated by the state.[24]

THE COMPOSITE CRISIS PHASE—AND STATE-INITIATED RESEARCH

We have not quite finished the story of the sociologists (or for that matter of the social workers). Quantitatively they came to prominence during what we have called the secondary crisis phase, characterised by social problems, whereby they received their symptom orientation and partly also their legitimating function. But during the late 1960s and the early 1970s their orientation toward applied interests of the state was not yet quite complete. To a certain extent they were still 'free' researchers, the resources for 'free' research still being fairly adequate.

---

[23] As of 2004: When these lines were written, my supposition was that the sociologists and social workers were becoming strongly silenced by structural features of their workplace, in the state and public administration in a wide sense. Recently, this has been given strong support by a large study of social workers. It is a three-year project headed by the sociologist Rolv Lyngstad, associate professor at Bodø College. The study, which at the time of writing is in its concluding phase, has looked into how social workers work and legitimise their profession. Many social workers are critical of the systems which their clients encounter, but the criticism 'remains on an ideological level', says Rolv Lyngstad in an interview in *Embla* (a Norwegian social work journal, No. 2, 2004). 'In actual work practice this [the criticism] is difficult to trace. [The critical stand] often becomes both narrow and oriented toward individuals. While one is taught [at the colleges] that poverty to a large extent is a product of social forces, and may be prevented, there is in practice little time for prevention.' The journal comments *inter alia* that 'he [Lyngstad] ... finds it paradoxical that the social workers to such an extent do their job without asking more questions concerning the administration (*styringen*) of society'. The article as a whole has the title 'Subservient Social Workers'. Other social workers are quoted as saying, 'We must become the advocates of the clients, like we were in the '70s and '80s', and 'The social work offices take the role of the clients' advocate to a much smaller extent than they should'. Note that Lyngstad's project is comparative, involving Norway, the US, Canada, Russia and Australia, and that preliminary results suggest a more subservient role on the part of Norwegian social workers than of social workers in the other countries.

[24] It should be emphasised that professions other than the three I have treated here may probably be discussed from the same general point of view. The general perspective of the present chapter is that the professions developed as 'replies' to the societal problems; that is, to problems which are of such a character that the established systems no longer fill their functions, whereupon the political legitimacy of the regime is threatened. The non-academic professions of engineers and teachers in the 1800s are cases in point. About the teachers, see Tove Stang Dahl, *Child Welfare and Social Defence*. Norwegian University Press 1985 (first edition in Norwegian 1978), Part IV.

As a parallel to this, the signs of political silencing in the profession had not yet developed full scale. Sociology was still a critical discipline.

Crises occurring together

This changed during the 1970s. We witnessed a fourth phase—to some extent coinciding with the third, secondary crisis phase discussed above—which may be designated the complex or *composite crisis phase* in the development of capitalist society. To some extent it is correct to say that the preceding phases of development succeeded each other. During the beginning of the fourth phase, towards the late 1970s, features of the preceding crises to a great extent occurred together, constituting a composite pattern. The law began to appear insufficient to maintain confidence, the economy wavered, social problems continued to worry, and new mass media trends which now were becoming apparent—with great emphases on crime and general entertainment—implied a focus on the issues in a new way. [25]

It is during this composite phase that applied state research in its true sense—research systematically financed and initiated by the state—developed as a main tendency in sociology. The seemingly everlasting expansion of the universities and research councils in their original form ended abruptly. At the same time, the resources available directly from the state (that is, from the ministries) for research and enquiry grew. In 1977, the various ministries had at their disposal about 35m Norwegian crowns—a lot of money at that time—for research and enquiries 'with the specific aim of illuminating problems confronting public administration'. It may be mentioned that the parallel amount

---

[25] As of 2004: David Garland has recently given an account of the noticeable changes in criminal policy – from a welfare orientation to punitiveness – which occurred at this time, see his *The Culture of Control*, Oxford University Press 2001. For an emphasis on the importance of the media in the process, see Thomas Mathiesen, 'Television, Public Space and Prison Population', *Punishment and Society*, Vol. 3 No. 1, 2001 and Gray Cavender, 'Media and Crime Policy: A Reconsideration of David Garland's *The Culture of Control*', *Punishment and Society* Vol. 6 No. 3, 2004.

As of 2004 the question may be raised whether we are still in a 'composite crisis phase' of development, as 'crisis' is defined earlier in this chapter (see note 8). Important signs of increasing deviance are still here, even if some trends have flattened out. More importantly, in quite a few countries very large numbers of industrial jobs have disappeared, and the British, French, German, American and Scandinavian economies have a hard time creating new positions to take their place. In Norway in 2003, an average of 50 jobs disappeared every day, while the unemployment rate increased and large companies moved their production out of the country, to low cost countries. Jobs in the service and information technology industries have not been able to catch up (also many jobs in information technology have been moved to low cost countries; source: Per Egil Hegge: 'Arbeidsplasser på flyttefot' (Work Places on the Move), *Aftenposten* 2 March 2004). There are also other signs of crisis: We live in a bewildering and complex economic, social and cultural world, with strong signs of influence and influx from the world around us. Globalisation is placed squarely on the agenda. Conflicts between the international or global and the national spheres arise, for example in law. In many ways we live in a risk society, where the roads ahead are uncertain, see Ulrich Beck, *World Risk Society*, Polity Press 1999. Beck believes that globalisation and our 'risk society' have fundamental repercussions in our national welfare systems. He calls our age 'the second modernity', characterised by 'globalisation, individualisation, gender revolution, underemployment and global risks (as ecological crises and the crash of global financial markets). The real theoretical and political challenge of the second modernity is the fact that society must respond to all these challenges *simultaneously*.' (p. 2). These bewildering and complex tendencies are not easily governed on the basis of old models of government, while new models have not yet come about. Together, the concept of 'composite crisis' fits the facts well.

in 1968 was 915,000 Norwegian crowns. In 1977, the Ministry of Communal Affairs and the Ministry of Environmental Protection each had at their disposal about 8m crowns, the Ministry of Social Affairs had a little over 6m crowns. About two-thirds of the projects were carried out at traditional research institutions—where state funds made their entry into the 'free' institutes—and about half of the appropriations went to social science projects.[26] Taken together, toward the end of the 1970s these circumstances forced a significant number of sociologists with research aspirations—and entire research institutes—into a corner, from which the only way out and to survival in research was an increased engagement in research financed by the state.[27]

---

[26] Information from *En oversikt over departementets prosjektbevilgninger til forskning, forsøk og utredningsarbeid m.v.* (A Review of Project Grants to Research, Experiments and Enquiries etc. from the Ministries), Norwegian Social Science Research Council 1977.

[27] As of 2004: Today, the processes leading up to the silent silencing of sociologists discussed above are still here, only more so. Let us look at it historically:

The Norwegian Research Council for Science and the Humanities (*Norges almenvitenskapelige forskningsråd*) was established in 1949, right after World War II. It gave research grants *inter alia* to social scientists, and was in great part financed through state lottery profits, which gave it a relatively free position. But as state interest in applied social research developed, this left its imprint on the research policy, and in 1977 a large department for social planning was established—like a Trojan horse, if you didn't like it—within the Council for Science and the Humanities. The department grew, and in 1987 it broke out and appeared as a full blown and separate Norwegian Council for Applied Social Research. This development shows the increasing significance of applied research in the social sciences.

But through the organizational structure in the 1980s, with the two separate councils, one old and one new, there was at least separate room for 'free' research in social science and the humanities through the old council. The latter had to be given its share in terms of funds. In 1993, however, five research councils (there were three others, largely irrelevant to social science) were amalgamated into one large Norwegian Research Council. The combined Norwegian Research Council of today is to a large extent financed directly by the state, and is outlining a number of research 'programmes' which research must fit into. The programmes are of interest to the state. The notion of applied research has become a powerful and active motive force throughout the large council. Symbolically, when you apply for a research grant, you must always take care to specify the utility or usefulness of the project. The money allotted to 'free' research, outside the specified programmes, is extremely limited. So-called 'effect research' has a strong position, again symbolising the direction of research.

A good concrete example is the so-called *Welfare Programme – Society, Family, Adolescence*, under the auspices of the Norwegian Research Council and largely financed by the state. In terms of funding it is one of the largest research efforts of the council. In its second phase, it is supposed to last from 2004-8. In a preparatory memorandum from the council of 28 June 2004, the strongly applied character of the programme, geared towards research useful for the state and centrally located decision makers, is very clear indeed. Proposers of projects which are not viewed as useful from the point of view of the state may as well not apply. For example, on p. 6 in the memorandum it is stated that the resources which are distributed

shall prepare the best possible store of knowledge with the purpose of evaluations and decisions in the political system, primarily in the central administration. The ministries allot significant sums to the research community, trusting that the research which is undertaken has a high relevance for their tasks. The research community must show understanding for this need.

Elsewhere the memorandum states that researchers must develop *inter alia* 'a greater consciousness on the part of researchers to the effect that knowledge must not only be developed, but also [be] organized so that it may be used by decision makers' (p. 9). The goal of research directly useful for public administration, and not 'fixedly academic' research (p. 7), permeates the memo. 'The legitimate demand for utility value on the part of the financial sources' is emphasised. At the same time, large projects are given priority over project plans from individual researchers, which receive low priority.

Research producing silence

State-initiated research has a tendency to produce silence as far as criticism of the state is concerned. More precisely, the selection of topics and issues, as well as conclusions, becomes more cautious. This does not mean that the research and planning sections of the ministries openly impose on researchers specific questions which they have to concentrate on (even if this also happens). The process of silencing is more subtle, and therefore more unnoticeable and dangerous. What happens in such a process is that particular areas of research are marked for research by the state. The contracts which are offered are frequently of a brief duration. Sociologists apply for funds to carry out research in these areas, and on these conditions, and they adapt themselves to implicit, unarticulated, but nevertheless strong expectations concerning the formulation of problems etc. Thereby, the research activity appears 'free' on the surface, while it is actually committed and bound. And it becomes more committed and bound as

While 'fixedly academic' research is hardly a solution to the dilemmas of sociological research (see below, the section on 'Flight into Abstractions?'), and while the 'utility value' of research may be a legitimate goal, the major question is of utility for whom. One thing is utility value 'from below', from broadly speaking the clients' perspective, quite another thing is utility value 'from above', from the perspective of financial sources and administrative decision makers in the central administration. This important distinction is discussed below (see the sections on 'A Generalized control crisis' and 'Research as seen from below'). The whole thrust is quite clearly in the latter direction, as the memorandum mentioned here clearly shows.

So much for the thinking in the Norwegian Research Council. As regards financial support for social research from the various ministries, the thinking is quite similar. In addition, major ministries have now begun to shift policy: They do not accept applications for research money, but invite tenders for the supply of research on issues formulated by the ministries. A major point is the price level, which may be set low. Tenders which for professional reasons exceed the price level substantially are easily turned down and do not get the job.

We can substantiate the situation of social research a bit further: In 1999, the last year for which we have figures, 23 per cent (457m N. crowns) of the running expenses (*driftsutgifter*) to 'research and evaluations' (the latter meaning practically oriented research) in the social sciences at the universities, colleges and research institutes came from *the ministries and the administrative counties.* 24 per cent (473m N. crowns) came from *the Norwegian Research Council.*; and 39 per cent (764m N. crowns) were for *basic budgets at the universities and colleges.* The remaining 14 per cent came from non-public sources, including private companies (*næringsliv*) with seven per cent.

We notice that the percentage going directly to the universities and colleges—39 per cent—is the largest. On the face of it, this looks promising. However, over half of the running expenses for research and evaluations in the social sciences at the universities were *salaries*, about one-third was *overheads*, and *only ten per cent were* so-called *running research expenses* (source: Kaja Wendt: *Ressursinnsatsen i samfunnsvitenskapelig forskning* (Resources to Research in the Social Sciences), Norsk institutt for studier av forskning og utdanning (NIFU), Skriftserie no. 29, 2001). This means that to a large extent the basic budgets in the social sciences going directly to the universities went to standard 'upkeep' of the institutions; only a relatively small amount of money actually went to free social research. The main sources for actual research are the various ministries and the Norwegian Research Council, where freedom is restricted and personal adjustments on the part of researchers are very likely to take place.

To repeat, the percentage of money flowing from private companies to the social sciences is small (but large in other fields of research). More private money would hardly help. What would help, and slow silent silencing down, would be much more money allotted directly to research at the universities and colleges, as permanent large yearly allowances without any strings attached to the various departments and institutes. More about this below.

To be sure, the ivory towers and the 'closed chambers' of the universities contain their own important problems and pressures with a silencing potential (see Tor Hernes: 'Myten om den rene og nøytrale forskning' (The Myth about Pure and Neutral Research), *Aftenposten* 7 March 2004). But being closer to the 'grass roots' of social research, the pressures would be easier to neutralise.

time goes on: over time, researchers and the research institutes are made dependent on continued appropriations.

The fact that the subtle character of the influence makes others believe that research is still 'free' is one thing. Another is the fact that it also makes the sociologists themselves believe this: because the process of influence is relatively inexplicit, the sociologists are lured into believing that as long as they have a well worked out plan for their research, a plan which they presumably can 'stand on'/stick to/stand by, their engagement in social research financed by the state constitutes little or no danger. However, the subtle process of influence, consisting of unspoken but strong expectations, begins even before the area of research has been chosen and the general problem has been formulated, and it continues independently of the well worked out as well as the detailed plan, because it is a question of economic survival: it simply is a question of bread and butter for the researcher, something which it is hard indeed to sacrifice on the altar of the well worked out plan and the clear line. The individual researcher changes his or her statement of the research question, and other formulations, in a correspondingly subtle way, and the research institutions do the same on behalf of their researchers. The subtle, very silent process of influence simultaneously makes this adjustment possible without major personal qualms: without the researcher having to be concerned with adjustment, in fact without his or her having to confront—and become subjectively aware of—the pronounced adjustment which in fact is taking place.

The subtle process of influence which is suggested here fits into the series of *noiseless forms of control*—unstated political control in the job situation rather than unambiguous *Berufsverbot*, secret and therefore undemonstrable surveillance rather than open political control—which is one characteristic of state control. The noiseless control of state research policy creates less opposition, fewer choice situations which may lead to conclusions negative to the state, less political consciousness and more rationalising in the psychological sense of the word, than the noisy forms of control.

Three further features

From the silenced social research in the composite crisis phase which in many ways is still with us follow some further features. Let me mention three which I believe are particularly important.

In the first place, a 'rationalisation' of research training is taking place. To some extent, the rationalisation follows the American Ph. D pattern. Research training of this kind is adapted to the demand for applied research. Typically, in a memorandum on the establishment of a programme for research training in Norway, from the Social Science Research Council, it is stated that 'in addition to the interest in basic research [research training should] place greater emphasis on meeting the demand for applied research'.[28]

---

[28] As of 2004: Today, research training at the Norwegian universities is even more in line with the American Ph. D pattern, and there has been a shift in the market direction. But the shift makes for more rather than less subservience on the part of university personnel, and certainly social scientists at the universities:

The doctoral degree is, in fact, called Ph. D. In the autumn of 2003 university education as a whole was reformed in an American direction, with Bachelor, Master and Ph. D. degrees. The old, European 'scholarly' emphasis has disappeared. The reform is officially named 'the quality

Secondly, and as a parallel, planning and public administration are becoming important course subjects in the social sciences at the universities and colleges. Planning and public administration draw on several different backgrounds, so that we begin to see a certain fusion of various types of social science into a general 'societal planning profession', adapted to the composite crisis features in our phase of the development.[29]

Thirdly, and as a further parallel, a certain influx of social scientists in state administration itself takes place. Quantitatively, the lawyers in particular but also the economists are of course still ahead, but in view of the brief history of social sciences in Norway the influx is not entirely insignificant. Obviously, the rationalised training programmes and the general planning orientation mentioned above fit well into this takeover.[30]

A generalised control crisis

At this point, important questions have to be raised: Is all applied research necessarily bad? Is all state initiated research activity necessarily negative?

Of course not. 'Applied research' is a catch-all category—covering everything from finding solutions to get poor people out of their difficult situation to providing large scale industry with methods for maximising productivity and thereby profit. And state initiated research is, at least in principle, an equally broad category. An evaluation of applied state initiated research is precisely that: a question of values.

---

reform'. Actually, it is a 'quantitative reform'. A larger number of students are to be sluiced through the educational system in a shorter time. The universities will in future receive state money partly relative to the number of examinations which are taken and the number of research articles which are published in high status journals and other venerable publication channels. This is in line with a general market oriented development in the public sector, for example the hospital sector, where hospitals are to receive money according to achievement, that is, the number of patients treated. Such market orientation might work in a perfect market, but in practice in the public sector it has several unexpected and undesirable consequences: In the universities the temptation will be great to adjust the pass/fail levels so that more students pass their exams. For hospitals the temptation will be equally great to use diagnoses which imply greater costs and thus legitimise more state money. In any case, a streamlining of research is to be expected, with an orientation toward 'useful' research.

As this book was going to press, a Bill proposing changes in the University and College Act had just been published. A rather blunt proposal to change the universities and colleges into semi-private institutions was stopped by broad opposition from the rank and file in the institutions before the Bill was made public. But several more suave and less noticeable—more silent—proposals in the same general direction remain. The Bill emphasises the 'usefulness' of university training and research. The direction is now usefulness 'for trade and business purposes' ('for *næringsmessig anvendelse*'). The silencing potential of such a change will be considerable. An administrative model emphasising increased control from the top of the structure is also proposed. The model will make the task of producing results useful 'for trade and business purposes' more efficient. To a considerable extent the Bill is well in line with the market and profit ideology of our time, which is also made relevant for the public sector.

[29] As mentioned in note 18, in 2002 close to 28 per cent, between one-quarter and one-third, of those classified as political scientists held advanced degrees in public administration and organization, public policy and administration and social planning: 735 in exact figures.

[30] As of 2004 this development has continued. The lawyers, while still important in public administration, have been overtaken by social scientists in a broad sense. Political scientists and sociologists have become particularly important in public administration. The lawyers' monopoly has receded.

The problem as I see it, is that applied research today is defined and seen from the point of view of those in power, not from the point of view of those out of power. It is seen from above, not from below. Applied research as seen from above is not necessarily inconsistent with needs as they are seen from below. A state initiated project on prostitution is not necessarily inconsistent with the interests of the prostitutes: it may reveal their poverty, which is probably in the prostitutes' interests as they see it. But it may be inconsistent, at least in part: Prostitutes may be interested in, say, the kind of labour protection regulation which they have in some countries. The Norwegian government, at least, would not be interested in this. In practice there is a tendency, perhaps even a strong tendency, for applied research as seen from above to become inconsistent with interests as seen from below.

In general: the state needs research to improve its overall governance in various sectors of society. However, the way in which efficient government is carried out may well be at odds with needs as they are defined by people on the ground. People on the ground, at the grass roots, may define their situation and their needs in very different ways compared with the state.

This is the crux of the problem. Applied research is regularly seen from above, and just as regularly such research comes to be at odds with needs as seen from below. Applied research seen from below, focused on needs as defined at grass root level, is rare, though there are exceptions. Applied research is top heavy. Forty years ago, it was the other way around.

The top heavy applied research tendency, supplemented by the rationalised, planning-oriented professional development geared toward posts and positions in state bureaucracy has become a link in the state's reply to the composite crisis which we are now experiencing. While the initial crisis concerned confidence, the primary crisis the economy, and the secondary crisis social issues, we may say that the present composite crisis, comprising all of these features, is experienced as a generalised *control crisis*. (See also note 25 for a further characterization of critical developments of our time.)

Market forces have returned as major forces of development. 'The hidden hand' is again partly applauded. We see that in our everyday life. The state's role as a moderator of dysfunctional effects of market forces is weakened. But the state's role as a controller of human behaviour is not weakened. On the contrary, expectations of effective control are even stronger now than before. When confronting the present deep and confusing, highly complex signs of crisis, the *question of control over developments becomes central to the state and the various state sub-systems.*

In connection with the demand for control the sociologists are now advertising their services, like the lawyers and the economists before them. The first golden, critical age of sociology was long passed.

HOW TO DEFEND OURSELVES?

Finally, we should ask ourselves: if the development which is outlined here worries us, how should we relate to it? How should we defend ourselves against it?

Flight into abstractions?

There exists another, parallel tendency in social research which constitutes one reply to the expanding applied profile: a tendency toward highly abstract theoretical activity which it is difficult to utilise for the state as well as for opponents of the state. This alternative tendency, paler and in the shadow of the main tendency, is in part found at the universities.

The emphasis on theoretical work on a high level of abstraction is certainly not new in sociology. Those of us who are old enough remember the 1950s and the influence of Talcott Parsons. Clearly, the emphasis has strong motive forces beyond that of being a self-protective reaction to the main professional profile which now is developing in the social sciences. The point here is that the emphasis does not produce any more of a critical stance— again those of us who are old enough will also remember C. Wright Mills' quest for critical sociology in the face of theoretical abstractionism. A culture emphasising silenced, cautious opinion rather than critical opinion follows in the wake of abstractionism; a culture of theoretical caution develops. The culture of caution based on theoretical abstractionism makes those of us who are employed by the universities act and speak in a 'responsible' fashion. By journeying into abstraction, we avoid the absorption and subtle bending of opinion which researchers financed directly or indirectly by the state are exposed to. What we say is instead 'wrapped up' in abstractions (intended for the consumption of no one except other abstraction-oriented sociologists), which makes left-over critical opinions unrecognisable, and harmless in a time when it is dangerous to have dangerous opinions.

The tendency toward theoretical abstraction is therefore hardly an adequate reply to and defence against the main profile which is developing, even if theoretically based work has to be a significant and integrated ingredient in the reply. When the main profile is supplemented by this secondary tendency, it actually becomes only clearer that sociology—like law and economics earlier—is in the process of becoming an unthreatening discipline. And it becomes only clearer that a subject which could have represented a critical potential and a store of knowledge for a whole range of more or less 'weak' groups in their struggle for life in our society becomes either uncritical or simply irrelevant. Some years ago, sociology was viewed as the rebellious subject compared to law and economics. This is no longer the case, and the twin-tracked development, consisting of a main profile oriented toward applied research on the part of the state together with an abstractionist secondary tendency, weakens the rebellious potential still further.

This means that other methods are necessary if we are to maintain and expand the space which is left for independent, critical (of course theoretically based) social science activity. Let me briefly suggest five roads, none of which can be taken by everyone, but all of which must probably be taken by some.

Alternative culture

In the first place, it is important to raise the question of how inescapable the individual's dependence actually is on the main profile which is developing. In part, the dependence is material: to repeat, it concerns one's livelihood. But I believe that to a significant extent the dependence is also phenomenological in character, that is, a question of how the situation is defined.

In the professions enormous prestige is tied to being a successful research person. The main criterion of success seems to consist of the production of work which wins the recognition of the professional collective, coupled to the attainment of a permanent research post. Those who are not successful in these ways frequently seem to experience life as falling apart.

But life does in fact not fall apart for this reason: research reports which are professionally recognised are not the only thing that gives meaning to life, and the transfer to a permanent research post is not the only possible meaningful road. It is possible to receive recognition for what you write for example from a political milieu, outside the purely professional collective. And it is possible to view a research fellowship or grant as an important phase in your life, in which you are able to do something you think is worthwhile, without thinking that you have to do exactly the same thing for the rest of your life. I believe much would be gained in the direction of greater freedom in relation to the highly silencing forces we have discussed if the attitude, the definition of the situation, were altered in this way.

But if this is to succeed at all, this alternative road cannot be taken by the individual alone. With the exception of those who have a more or less inhuman personal strength—and very few of us have that—the individual standing alone will quickly become a victim of prevailing professional evaluations, whereby he or she will either submit or run into great troubles. It is essential that several people take the alternative road together. The implication is that when you are a group or a category with internal bonds, you may create an opposition, an alternative debate and joint reflection—in short, a culture against the prevailing definition of the situation.

Concrete organizing

However the development of such an alternative professional culture, a culture which may soften the individual's dependence on the professional profile which is now expanding, is in turn dependent on alternative concrete organizing taking place. This is the second main point and road which I wish to emphasise. As the situation is today, there are many sociologists who are frustrated and feel desperate over the development, but they are spread over the entire country, at various universities, colleges and institutes, without much organized interaction.

Organizing as a basis for the alternative culture should take place within the profession. It is possible to have a good deal of communication and organization within one's profession without extensive resources. But as pointed out in *Chapter 4*, organizing should probably also take place across the boundaries of the profession, to groups with similar views in related professions and to groups outside academia—for example, to client groups in need of counter-expertise. Some organizations of this kind already exist in Norway; within my own field of interests, I have personally experienced KROM (the Norwegian Prisoners' Organization) as one of them. And it is possible to establish others, on a short-term or long-term basis. The sociologists who wish to participate in work of this kind will have a common general frame of reference in the threat which the silencing main profile of the profession is creating.

Turning the money stream

But in the third place, and if we assume that a fair number nevertheless will continue with research, it is at the same time important to work actively— politically—to turn the stream of research money as much as possible directly towards the universities.

More precisely: it is not enough to say, as it is often said by sociologists, that the 'fundamental control' of projects must lie in the research institutions. It is not enough to say this because the silencing of opinions through the control of money is so imperceptible and subtle. The fundamental control of problems and projects may very well be maintained on paper, in the written contract, without actually existing in practice.

What the sociologists and social scientists generally should do is to present concrete demands concerning transfer to research funds—*for free use*—directly to the universities. A number of negative things may be said about social science at the universities—and I have said some of those things above—but nevertheless there is, at the universities, a certain room for political freedom of a type which the pragmatically oriented applied institutes we now see developing do not give room for. Such a turning of the money stream may thereby contribute to a loosening of the grip which is in the process of tightening around sociological research activity, and to a neutralising of the highly silencing tendencies.

I do not know to what extent such demands will succeed. But they will bring us further than no formulation of them. Therefore it is our duty to present them and to press for them, rather than to yield pragmatically to state arrangements.

Security

In the fourth place, it is important to work in a similarly active way, through political channels, against the 'day-to-day' or 'month-to-month' labour system in research which now has had a chance to develop.

As mentioned above, the dependence of social scientists on the main profile in the profession is in an important sense material. Short-term contracts, with the high degree of insecurity which they produce, increase the tendency toward silence. It is only in an ideal world that an insecure material situation may be viewed as a productive factor in critical science.

Research as seen from below

Finally, and as implied above, it is of vital importance to raise anew research as seen from below, taking as our point of departure the interests of those out of power rather than those in power, those who are repressed rather than those who repress, those who are governed rather than those who govern, those who lack channels of communication to and influence over decision-making bodies and institutions rather than of those who have such channels and, in fact, are these bodies and institutions.

What I have said here has been said before. It is a part of yesterday's ideology. But today it sorely needs to be repeated and revitalised. Such a programme raises many difficult questions, *inter alia* questions concerning the relations and possible conflicts between interests seen from below, which in turn raise questions of choice between values. We should not let ourselves be paralysed by these questions, which often are raised by those who favour the main stream. Rather than hesitate, we should go ahead and make a start, and reflect on, discuss and solve the questions as they come along.

It implies going against the stream, and against the wishes of the money sources. But, keeping in mind the possibility of developing an alternative research culture, and the possibility of making a joint effort, it is a challenging task. In fact, it is possible to envisage an alternative applied research culture, systematically oriented to and voicing interests, perspectives and understandings from *below*. Although we cannot make the forces of state oriented applied research disappear as if by magic, we can at least make some headway in the alternative direction.

It would involve taking the first points outlined earlier in this section of the chapter seriously.

*

In other words, it is possible to do something with the situation. It follows from the main argument of this chapter that society never generates professions which are revolutionary in relation to that society. In their opening phases the professions may be oppositional, and within their frameworks individuals may be quite resistant, but as *professions* they quiet down when they grow large and receive important societal functions. I have tried to analyse some of the reasons for this above. But this does not mean that those of us who have entered a profession may not do something with our situation, create room for action, retain and develop our critical sense.

If we fail to do this, we neglect to utilise the opportunities which do exist.

6   Political Surveillance and Public Arena

CHAPTER 6

Political Surveillance and Public Arena

On 25 November 1977, a new set of instructions for the surveillance activities of the Norwegian police was adopted by the Government. The Government also decided that in contrast to the old instructions, the new instructions were to be made public.[1]

The adoption of the instructions was of course immediately made known through our various mass media. The general coverage says a great deal about how 'the bourgeois public arena' functions in contexts like this. [2]

In this chapter I shall describe important features of the coverage. The coverage contained four elements: the newspaper announcements, a press release from the Norwegian News Agency, a press release from the Ministry of Justice and the instructions themselves. By analysing the interplay between these four elements we gain an understanding of how the instructions, through various rhetorical twists, were made to appear much more reassuring and politically unthreatening than warranted. The coverage also provides a background to understanding *inter alia* some aspects of the lawyers' relation to political activity.

---

[1] As of 2004: Since this essay was written (1978), instructions for the surveillance activities of the Norwegian surveillance police (today called the 'Police Security Service') have been changed, to some extent following criticism of the kind illustrated in this chapter. Today's instructions were adopted on 19 August 1994. The most significant change is this: While the instructions of 25 November 1977 (the starting point for this chapter) stated that membership of a legal political organization or participation in a legal political activity could not 'in itself' constitute a basis for the obtaining and registering of information about an individual, today's instructions flatly state that 'Membership in political or other legal organization or activity does not constitute a basis for obtaining or registering information' (§ 4, 2 passage in today's instructions). In other words, the words 'in itself' have been taken out, which obviously is a significant change.

On the other hand, the present instructions too are wide and discretionary. Notably, § 4 of the present instructions states that the surveillance service is obliged to gather information about persons, groups and organizations 'which may be suspected' of 'preparing or undertaking' a long string of vaguely defined acts against the security and independence of the state. Persons, groups and organizations 'which may be suspected' of preparing or undertaking something may indeed be a wide category.

I reprint the present essay here without introducing details about today's instructions in the text partly because the current instructions, with the important exception mentioned above, still constitute a highly discretionary instrument, but above all because the essay deals with general questions about how for example such instructions are handled in public by political authorities and parts of the media.

[2] With the expression 'bourgeois public arena' I attempt to translate the German concept of *bürgerliche Öffentlichkeit*, or the Norwegian *borgerlig offentlighet*, into English. It designates a presumed openness to general observation: a field where matters and issues are presumably open to inspection and discussion. The particular *bourgeois* 'public arena' may be said to have developed from the late 1700s onwards, beginning with the coffee-houses and saloons as *bourgeois* meeting places, and ending in the large present-day mass media. See Jürgen Habermas, *Strukturwandel der Öffentlichkeit*, Luchterhand 1962.

THE NEWSPAPER PRESENTATION

The adoption of the new instructions was given its first extensive coverage in the evening issue of the large daily *Aftenposten* on the very day of the adoption. The Government adopted the instructions at 12 p.m. that day, and *Aftenposten* got the story because it was the only paper with an evening issue. Most people receive their information about a phenomenon like this through newspapers and other similar media; only very few probe further into background press releases or for that matter to the source itself. Therefore, the newspaper's first presentation is important and formative of people's opinions.

In the above-mentioned evening issue of *Aftenposten*, the paper claimed in a five column front page headline: 'Political surveillance clearly forbidden, strict rules about professional secrecy'. This, then, was the first impression of the new instructions which the paper's approximately 200,000 subscribers at the time received. In a similar tone, the first point made in the article itself was that 'Membership in a legal political organization or legal political activity cannot in itself constitute a basis for the obtaining and registering of information. This is established in clear words in the new instructions for the surveillance service of the police …' All of it sounded very reassuring. Furthermore, the article stated

> with regard to the permission to surrender information to others, it is emphasised that information from the surveillance service may only be surrendered to others when this is necessary to avert an immediate danger to the security of the Realm, or someone's life, health, freedom, or property. This concerns information to public authorities as well as to private parties.

This sounded even more reassuring and restrictive, and with these introductory words the part of the article set in large print ended. The rest of the article as a whole held the same general tone. In such a context it sounded only reasonable that

> the surveillance service shall obtain information about persons, groups and organizations which *inter alia* may be suspected of preparing or undertaking actions which may entail a danger to the security of the Realm, to the Constitution or the Head of State, and to the general order and peace. In addition are included all activities involving intelligence activity, infiltration, sabotage, and terrorism which may involve a danger to the security of the Realm.

Corresponding headlines and statements in large print in a series of other newspapers were similarly reassuring. The Norwegian News Agency, NTB, sent out its own press release about the issue. In *Stavanger Aftenblad*, which based its coverage on this press release, it was stated in a four column headline: 'Careful Consideration in the Surveillance Service', in *Tønsberg Blad* it was stated (over four columns): 'New Public Instructions: Prohibits Political Surveillance', in *Dagningen* it was stated (over three columns): 'New Instructions for Surveillance made Public: No Registration of Legal Activity', in *Arbeiderbladet* it was stated (over three columns): 'New Instructions for the Surveillance Police—Legal Political Activity No Basis for Surveillance', in *Hamar Dagblad* it was stated (four columns): 'Instructions Contain Clear Prohibition Against all Political Surveillance'. And so on.

I have carried out a simple content analysis of all the newspaper headlines in Norway which announced the new instructions. Editorials, commentaries, etc. are not included—I have only included the regular news coverage. The material has been gathered by Norsk Argus A/S, and may be viewed as complete. In all, 44 regular news items were published about the instructions during the days following 25 November. As many as 15 of these had what I would call a 'clearly reassuring' form—they were formed as the examples given above. Twenty-six headlines had what should perhaps be called a 'neutral' form, for example 'Instructions for Police Surveillance Adopted', 'The Surveillance Instructions are made public', 'The Surveillance Police get Instructions for their Work'. Only *three* of the 44 headlines gave the impression that the new instructions in one way or another did not provide sufficient control of the surveillance police (e.g. *Arbeideravisa*: 'Instructions for Surveillance: Suspicion a Condition for Surveillance of Individuals'). At the same time it is important to recognise that many of the 26 headlines which I thought should be designated as 'neutral', did have a touch of something reassuring (while none of them had any touch of antagonism): expressions like 'Instructions for Police Surveillance Adopted' and 'Instructions for Surveillance made Public' suggest that clear limits are set and that the period of secretiveness is over. In addition, it is important to recognise that most of the latter headlines—and two of the three headlines which gave the impression that the instructions were not satisfactory—were followed by highly reassuring texts in the actual articles.

As indicated above, the highly reassuring presentation and tendency of the newspapers was to a large extent based on a press release from the Norwegian News Agency NTB. In turn, this was based on a press release from the Ministry of Justice. The former press release—the one from NTB—was a slight re-writing and abbreviation of the Ministry's release. In addition, it differed from the Ministry's release in one important respect: because of some particulars of presentation, the NTB release was slightly more 'reassuring' in form than the original press release from the Ministry of Justice. Particularly important in this respect is the fact that the NTB press release—in contrast to the press release from the Ministry—used a separate, independent paragraph when emphasising that membership of legal political organizations etc. cannot in itself provide a basis for surveillance. This way of presenting the material provided a particularly good basis for 'reassuring'—or at least neutral—newspaper stories.

LAYERS OF THE ONION

We may regard the newspaper coverage as the outermost layer of the 'onion', and NTB's press release as the next. If we probe into the third layer, which is the press release from the Ministry of Justice, we come slightly closer to the heart. But only slightly, because also this layer is thick—if you wish to remain with the metaphor.

Unlike the instructions themselves, the Ministry's press release opens by telling something presumably very reassuring: that during the preparation of the instructions, the Government has undertaken a very painstaking evaluation of the security interests of the Realm on the one hand, and on the other hand considerations of legal protection and the possibility that the surveillance service may happen to commence surveillance of individuals or organizations on an unsound basis.

It sounds additionally reassuring—at least to non-lawyers—when the Ministry's release immediately continues by relating that the instructions 'are to serve as a basis for the work of the surveillance service, and indicate the limits of its activity'. And what, then, is the task of the surveillance service? According to the instructions this is, the Ministry's press release continues,

> to prevent and counteract all crimes to the extent that these may entail a danger to the security of the Realm. The surveillance service is also to prevent and counteract infiltration, sabotage, attacks, etc. and illegal intelligence activity.

All of it sounds ever so restricted and—again—reassuring.

With regard to the question of the task of the surveillance service, it is very interesting to compare the Ministry's press release with the actual instructions themselves—the onion's heart. In §2, the instructions list as many as five comprehensive chapters in the Penal Code: chapter 8 on crimes against the independence and security of the State; chapter 9 on crimes against Constitution and the Head of State; chapter 12 on crimes against public authorities; chapter 13 on crimes against general order and peace; and chapter 14 on dangerous crimes of a general kind (*allmenfarlige forbrytelser*)—in addition to a good deal of specialised legislation. These chapters, which in other words are referred to without any delimitation and as totalities, include provisions which clearly concern political opinions (the insulting of foreign heads of state, defamation of the King, defamation of our Constitution, etc.) and in addition—as indicated already—provisions which have to do with the general order and peace. These are violations of law to which the surveillance service, according to the instructions, is to devote 'special' attention—with a view toward 'prevention and counteraction'.[3]

Let us switch back to the Ministry's release. 'Furthermore', we are told, 'the surveillance service shall *inter alia* give assistance and advice during the implementation of security measures in state administration and in public and private activities which are of importance to the security of the Realm, as well as provide information about persons in cases of security clearance'. Most reassuring, the reader must feel.

---

[3] As of 2004: These chapters in the penal code have recently been reviewed by a committee appointed by the Ministry of Justice. The committee has prepared a new set of paragraphs partly excluding some of those mentioned in the text above, which probably will come into force as law in 2004 or 2005.

In § 1 of the surveillance instructions of 19 August 1994, which supplanted the instructions discussed here, the same kinds of criminal acts are referred to, but more briefly, in addition to more 'modern' crimes like 'illegal technological transfer, diffusion of weapons of mass destruction, sabotage and politically motivated violence (terrorism)'. The brevity of the acts referred to in the present instructions as well as the rather vaguely defined 'modern' crimes if anything provide the surveillance authorities with more rather than less discretion than in former times.

Again it is interesting to compare with the actual instructions. The providing of 'assistance' and 'advice' of the kinds mentioned above, which are only mentioned briefly and in passing in the press release, appears to be a very comprehensive task in the instructions themselves. I refer to §3 of the instructions which reads as follows:

The surveillance agencies shall:
a) at any time keep the Ministry of Justice informed of all circumstances important for the internal security of the Realm
b) within the regulations of law and superior instructions, lead and co-ordinate the surveillance service in the country as a whole, by *inter alia* giving general and special directives for the execution of the service and the choice of priorities between tasks, by giving information, guidance, and help to the regional and local surveillance service, and by participating in investigations of criminal acts mentioned in § 2 [see the comprehensive content of §2 listed above, T.M.]
c) co-operate with the military security and intelligence service, and give the military authorities information concerning circumstances of importance for military security and preparation
d) give guidance and advice in connection with the implementation of security measures in the state administration, the railways, the mail service, the telegraph and communication service in general, the merchant marine, the airways, the electricity supply, and public and private industries of importance for the security and state of readiness of the Realm, and implement special measures to surveil and prevent acts in these fields as mentioned in §2
e) provide personal information in connection with the security clearances
f) operate as central adviser and warning agency and provide investigatory assistance in connection with sabotage and terrorist actions
g) establish and maintain contact with police authorities, and the surveillance- and security services, of other countries
h) establish, maintain, and re-organize countrywide archives and registers as mentioned in §5, see also § 4 2nd section
i) be in charge of the training of surveillance service personnel.

Once again back to the Ministry's press release, which continues as follows: 'The instructions contain limitations on the surveillance service's opportunity to obtain information about persons, groups, and organizations'. Most certainly such limitations are introduced, the reader must think. 'The principle is,' the release continues, 'that such information is only to be obtained and registered when suspicion exists [*foreligger*] that acts which may mean a danger to the security of the Realm are being prepared or undertaken'. These sentences are very interesting if we once again compare with what the instructions themselves say. In §4, 1st section, it is stated: 'The surveillance service is to obtain information about persons, groups, and organizations which may be suspected [*kan mistenkes*] of preparing or undertaking acts mentioned in §2'. In other words, the provision is—in the actual instructions—positively formulated, and information is to be obtained when persons, groups, and organizations 'may be suspected [*kan mistenkes*]' of preparing or undertaking the acts in question, not only 'when suspicion in fact exists [*foreligger*]'. The difference, of course, is great.

And still this is not the end. Immediately following the sentence in the Ministry's press release which says that 'information is only to be obtained and registered when suspicion exists', the release continues with the following two sentences and without a new paragraph:

> Furthermore, information which is obtained in connection with security clearances may be registered and stored if it is assumed that the information may be of significance later. It has been decided that membership in legal political organizations, or legal political activity, in itself cannot provide a basis for the obtaining and registering of information.

The first of these two sentences—which is obviously a very important sentence—is in other words opened by a 'furthermore,' as if the sentence simply continues the reassuring principle that 'information is only to be obtained and registered when suspicion exists'. But the sentence in question is obviously not a continuation of this principle, rather quite the contrary. In addition, the sentence is inserted just before the highly reassuring sentence that membership of legal political organizations, or legal political activity, cannot 'in itself' provide a basis for surveillance. The totality of it is, in other words, a highly trustworthy and reliable impression.

So is the totality of the rest of the Ministry's press release. Below I quote the rest of it *in extenso*—thereby the reader has actually read the press release as a whole:

> The instructions also contain more precise regulations of the use of information on the part of the surveillance service. The principle here is that information about persons is to be provided neither to public authorities nor to private parties without there being a legal basis for it, or without its following from the tasks which the surveillance service is to attend to according to instructions. Among other things, information may be provided when it is necessary to avert an immediate danger to the security of the Realm or to someone's life, health, freedom, or property.
>
> Civil servants in the surveillance service have to abide by professional secrecy. The duty of professional secrecy also holds in relation to police officers who are not tied to the surveillance service.
>
> It has been decided that the general instructions for the surveillance service of the police are to be a public document. The instructions will be included in *The Norwegian Publication of Legal Regulations*. For your information, a copy of the instructions is enclosed with this press release.
>
> More detailed regulations concerning the organization and internal division of complete etc. of the surveillance service have simultaneously been drawn up. The plan for the organizational structure of the surveillance service which was presented in White Paper No. 89 (1969-70), has been followed up and developed further. Since there are indications suggesting that intelligence activities are being performed against the surveillance service and its personnel, the regulations concerning the organization etc. of the surveillance service are graded as security material.

This highly pacifying statement may again be compared with the innermost layer of the 'onion', the heart: the surveillance instructions themselves. Partly as a summary of what I have said above, I refer particularly to the facts

- that membership of a legal political organization, or legal political activity, cannot 'in itself' provide a basis for the obtaining and registering of information—whereby such membership, or such activity, of course may constitute a very important *part* of the basis for registration [not mentioned at all in the Ministry's press release];

- that the surveillance service, as mentioned above, is to obtain information about persons, groups, and organizations which hypothetically 'may be suspected' of 'preparing or undertaking' actions which 'may entail' a danger to the security of the Realm;
- that the surveillance service, as mentioned above, is to devote 'special' attention to acts which are covered by five great chapters in the Penal Code, including many provisions about political 'opinions';
- that the Surveillance Agency is to co-operate with a long series of other authorities—among others military security and intelligence service—as well as with public and private industries 'of importance for the security and the state of preparation of the Realm', so that the total network of organizations in which the surveillance authorities enter is to be comprehensive and tightly knit; and
- a great deal more which shows the discretionary authority which is assigned to the surveillance authorities.

In all, there is good reason to conclude that the guarantee against political surveillance, emphasised with greater pride the further away from the onion's heart you come, is in reality simply not present.[4]

PUBLIC ARENA—THE GENERAL ONE

What, then, is illustrated by the relationship between the surveillance instructions, the press release of the Ministry of Justice, the press release of the News Agency, and the headlines and coverage in general of the newspapers?

---

[4] As of 2004: This proved to contain a prediction which was quite correct. In 1994 an official commission, named the 'Lund Commission' after its head, Supreme Court Justice Ketil Lund, was set up by Parliament to investigate the activities of the secret services. The commission, which published its report in 1996, revealed very extensive political surveillance, especially of left wingers and members of left wing political parties and organizations (illegal telephone tapping, room bugging (which was and still is illegal in Norway), illegal undercover surveillance, etc.) through a number of decades from 1945 on. *Notably, the period included many years after the instructions discussed in this chapter were introduced.* Major criticism occurred in the 1990s, and the files were opened for all who wanted to see whether they had been subjected to political surveillance. By January 2003 12,800 people had asked to see their files. A large number of people on the left of the political spectrum had illegal entries in their files. My own file contained a number of illegal entries. Many of them concerned newspaper articles on prison and criminal policy which I had written during the 1970s. One of them showed that I had been subjected to illegal undercover surveillance at a criminal policy conference organized by the Norwegian Prisoners' Organization, KROM. I was chairman of the organization at the time.

Parallelling this, also in the 1990s, proposals by an officially appointed committee in 1997 suggested a widening of the discretionary authority of the secret police (regarding telephone tapping and communications control in general, technical tracing and so on). The proposals were adopted with some amendments in 1999, and were in many ways integrated with the ongoing development of international/global surveillance activities through the Schengen Information System, The Europol Computer Systems, etc.; see references in note 2 in *Chapter 8* below. New terrorism legislation after 11 September 2001 widened discretionary authority still further.

The relationship illustrates in a particularly clear fashion how public administration, and the press, function as participants in the 'public arena' in our society—in effect as participants in a culture of presentation and argumentation where emphasis is placed on those forms of presentation and argumentation which accentuate and support powerful interests and views.

We pride ourselves in having a public administration which precisely is 'public'—we have an Act of Public Affairs and an Act of Administration which emphasise the opportunity of insight into the administrative system—and we pride ourselves in having a press which is 'free'. We feel reassured that what should be made known to us, is in fact made known for us, both from the administrative system directly and through the press. Both the administration's general apparatus for making issues public, as well as the organization of the press, are strengthened at precisely the same time: the administration gets its public information secretaries and its information departments, and the press (in Norway) its state support and its improved information techniques with which to counter a difficult market.

However, through the relationship revealed between the various links in the case discussed here, we see that this ideal picture does not correspond with the reality. In the first place, the surveillance instructions themselves are at important points formulated so that the lack of a guarantee against political surveillance—in many ways the core of the matter—is masked. Secondly, the lack of a guarantee is masked further by subtle shifts of emphasis and adjustments through the various press releases and in the newspapers themselves, so that the end result which reaches the public corresponds with the impression which the authorities, and the large main stream media, wish to give when it comes to basic societal issues of this kind: a reassuring impression which makes you 'calm down'.[5]

For years before the instructions of 1977 there was considerable 'unrest' around the issue of political surveillance, an unrest which raised fundamental questions concerning the legitimacy of the surveillance system, and of the criminal justice system in general. Attempts were made to criminalise the unrest, but the attempts were insufficient to subdue the feelings of doubt which had come to be associated with the surveillance service. However, a new set of surveillance instructions, with a smoother surface than the old set, presented to the public through steps such as those which I have suggested, subdued the unrest considerably. It is a striking fact that after the new set of surveillance instructions were made public on 25 November 1977, the debate concerning surveillance of political opinions to a considerable extent died down. As

---

[5] As of 2004: This is perhaps no longer quite so much the case for the media. After the end of party affiliation of Norwegian newspapers, and the development of a general market orientation of the media, the media are presumably more interested in debate and disagreement. It seems, however, that the media are more interested in this as entertainment which sells than as information. Criticism of surveillance activities may flare up, but dies down again quickly, and critique and discussion of the more complex aspects of surveillance, involving the international or global systems of control, are virtually non-existent; see *Chapter 8: Panopticon and Synopticon as Silencing Systems*. Also, in the age of modern terrorism, support for the surveillance activities of the police is, at least as far as Norway goes, almost unanimous throughout the mainstream media. In other words, the media still seem to mask the very real threats to civil liberties and legal rights.

indicated already, suave methods, a repertoire of minor but vitally important rhetorical twists and turns of phrase, made silence prevail.[6]

PUBLIC ARENA—THE LEGAL ONE

But the relationship between instructions, press releases, and newspaper presentations also illustrates something else. To me, at least, it illustrates the dangers involved in using legal arguments from a radical standpoint in connection with the issue of political surveillance.

The initiative to formulate new instructions for the surveillance service was taken against the background of some celebrated instances of political surveillance, and other news concerning the surveillance service, revealed during the mid-1970s.[7]

In the public debate which subsequently took place, and which ended in the adoption of the quieting instructions for the surveillance service discussed here, the nation's most well-known *lawyers*—on both sides of the issue—were among the foremost targets of interviews by the newspapers and other media. The lawyers were interviewed, they received coverage, and it was above all among and between them that *the* debate took place. In the heat of the debate one could in fact discern the contours of what may be called a *legal public arena* around the issue. The 'legal public arena',[8] which is a part of 'the bourgeois public arena', is a culture of argumentation where arguments of a legal or juridical kind are brought to the forefront. In connection with a wide variety of issues, the lawyers in Norwegian society are regularly interviewed as interesting participants, receiving coverage as people who are entitled to an opinion, and legal concepts, distinctions, and ways of reasoning are given an opportunity to leave their mark on given debates. These and not other concepts and ways of reasoning thus frequently formulate and define what the debates and the issues 'actually' involve.

One of these typically legal questions—and concepts—is the question and the concept of legal 'basis' or 'authority' (*hjemmel i lov*). For example, is *a basis or authority in law* necessary for all types of surveillance? Presumably, it is hard indeed to know: concerning this, there has been great discord among those learned in law. On the one hand, it has been maintained that registration of publicly accessible pieces of information—among them, political party activities—is not really 'surveillance', and does not presuppose a specific legal basis: registration of publicly accessible pieces of information is being performed by many people in our society—for example by the press. On the other hand, it has been maintained that the purpose of the registration performed by the surveillance service is very different from that of the press, and that 'the best reasons suggest' that a specific basis in law must be presupposed for such

---

[6]   As of 2004: Though silence prevailed for a time, unrest did return, culminating with the *Lund Report* and its aftermath, see note 4.

[7]   The most celebrated piece of news concerned a left-wing journalist who informed a newspaper that he was in the possession of lists of people employed by the surveillance police. He had gathered the information through an intelligent use of open sources. The statement led to the arrests of several people who were implicated, and to a great deal of public debate.

[8]   I owe this term to Mary-Ann Hedlund.

registration performed by the service. A very significant part of the debate in the mid-1970s, up until the instructions of 1977, in fact concerned this specific legal question.

I do not mean to say that the question of legal basis is politically unimportant. At specific junctures, the question of legality/illegality of activities on the part of the surveillance service and other public agencies may become very significant. We find many examples of this (see for example note 4 above, about the Lund Commission). However, I mean to say that when this question becomes overarching, and just about the only question raised by lawyers who monopolise the debate, the debate is greatly narrowed. The important political issue of whether we want a surveillance service at all, or whether we want a surveillance service with such a broad mandate as the surveillance instructions provide, is lost in the much narrower legal question of whether the surveillance service or the mandate given to it have a basis in law.

THREE FUNCTONS

The debate over 'legal basis', on the legal public arena, has three functions which I would like to point to.

Seemingly neutral
In the first place, through the debate over 'legal basis' the discussion becomes transformed or converted from being a clearly political debate—about, and for or against, surveillance—into being an exchange of opinion concerning a seemingly neutral and technical legal question.

Jurisprudence is also political, but it is given a clothing or coat of neutrality and technicality, so that the political aspects of the debate are lost from sight. The seemingly neutral legal question has a significant side-tracking effect on the actual political struggle. In general, it may be said that one of the functions of the lawyers (and especially of the professorial legal dogmatists) is that of being society's professional 'transformers' of politically controversial issues into seemingly neutral and technical questions of a less burning (and more professional and more inaccessible) character.

Acceptance
Secondly, through the debate over 'legal basis' the discussion concerning surveillance has been subtly transformed into a general acceptance of surveillance.

To repeat, the debate has not primarily concerned the issue of surveillance as such; rather, it has been argued that specific types of surveillance demand a basis in law, or that they do not have the necessary basis in law. Thereby, surveillance as such has tacitly become more or less accepted as a premise for discussion. The implication is that if it had a legal basis, things would be all right.

More acceptable legal basis
Thirdly, through the debate over 'legal basis' increased pressure has been brought to bear on the authorities to construct a better and more reasonable legal

basis for the political surveillance which in fact is taking place. *Here we are, in our context, at the heart of the matter.*

The lawyers participating in the debate, and, it should be noted, precisely those radical and well intentioned lawyers holding the view that a legal basis must be mandatory for every form of surveillance (e.g. also for registration of publicly accessible information such as party activities), actually participated *in pressing through a new, more neatly formulated, more acceptable legal basis—if not in the form of a new Act, at least in the form of the new instructions which we have discussed in this chapter.* The new legal basis is also more acceptable in that it could be made public. The old basis, the old set of instructions, were—strange as it may sound—formulated in such a way that people could not be allowed to see them.

As far as I can understand, lawyers may learn a great deal from the process which took place. It must be important for progressive lawyers who participate politically always to be aware of the danger that the legal debate and arguments may side-track the discussion from the core of the matter, and of the danger that the legal way of thinking and legal technique may in fact contribute to the production of a result which is the very opposite of the actual aim. If it is maintained that something requires a legal basis, or that is has a doubtful or dubious basis, or that it is simply not based in law, the danger is great—if the question is important enough—that a legal basis will simply be produced.

And the question of surveillance was more than important enough for such a basis to be produced. The debate followed suit. Silence prevailed.

7   A Meeting of Judges in Italy:
A Travel Account

CHAPTER 7

A Meeting of Judges in Italy: A Travel Account

It happened in Italy, but it could have occurred anywhere. In September 1977 I went on a two-week trip to Italy, with a beginner's course in Italian behind me, to participate in a conference on the right to strike. I had been informed about the conference through an announcement from the Ministry of Foreign Affairs. In view of the political developments in Italy, the subject interested me, and I hoped that my beginner's course would be of help.

I arrived in Perugia in Umbria, where the conference was to be held, on the day before the opening. The conference was arranged by the *Centro Internazionale Magistrati Luigi Severini*, with headquarters in *Palazzo di Guistisia*, and the first thing I did was therefore to find my way to this palace.

I came to *Palazzo di Guistisia* after working hours, but I understood quite quickly that the Justice Palace was the headquarters of the courts. I knocked on the door of an enormous office, and there sat a solitary judge, apparently working overtime. He spoke a little English, and explained that the conference— he was not himself going to participate—was to begin the day after. In the meantime, he recommended the best hotel in the town.

I found my way to the best hotel, not in order to find a room there—I didn't have money for that—but to find out if anyone there knew more about the conference. They did not. But they did know about me: a room was already booked for me. And it was immediately pointed out that *Centro Luigi Severini* paid for *everything*—food and drinks as well as the room. I was only to make myself comfortable.

This surprised me a little, but I gladly accepted. I went early to bed and slept well—after a good red wine—in a first class pre-paid room.

At 5 o'clock in the afternoon of the next day the conference began. It took place in a large conference building nearby, with a wonderful view of the city. As I walked into the conference hall, I understood for the first time that this was no joke. In the large assembly room—which more or less resembled the assembly hall of the Security Council in the United Nations' building—the various countries had separate seats for their delegations. I sat down on the seat where it said '*Norvegia*'. Next to me I found a sign saying '*Espania*'. Since it was before the fall of the Franco regime, this did not make me feel easier. But luckily, that seat remained empty.

The other seats, however, were gradually filled. Behind me sat Turkey, and onwards through my row: Japan, France, England, West Germany, Luxembourg, Holland, Belgium and a series of others. We sat in an enormous semi-circle. On the floor, inside the semi-circle, a number of chairs had been set out. Gradually the chairs were filled. Half of those people sitting inside the semi-circle wore uniforms, adorned with gold and ribbon in quantities which I had never seen before. On the podium, seven men in dark suits walked up and sat down. Behind the podium a number of people sat under the sign '*Stampa*'. I looked up in my dictionary to find what country this was. It turned out to be the press.

Then the seven men in dark suits began to speak, one after the other. They spoke about things which I had not learned in my beginner's Italian course. But it was clear that they hailed and applauded each other and the *Centro Luigi Severini* which had made this conference possible. One of the seven dark-suited men spoke for a particularly long time. He was a professor of jurisprudence, and gave what I understood to be a general talk on the right to strike in Italy. I understood he was worried, but did not understand why. When he had finished, he drew enormous applause from those inside the semi-circle, those with the gold and ribbons. I applauded politely myself, even if I had not understood so much. I noticed that several others from other countries also applauded politely, and thought that they had perhaps not understood so much either. A representative from Japan on my right hand-hand side had been nodding approvingly throughout the talk. I asked him in a whisper whether he understood Italian. Rather than nodding, a headshake was now the reply.

With this, the meeting was terminated for that day. The journalists ran to their telephones. The men in black suits looked very pleased. I went to my pre-paid hotel to have dinner with red wine. I looked forward to seeing the newspaper reports, because then I would perhaps understand a little more. And I looked forward to the following day, because then I expected a colleague from Norway to join me. His Italian was about as poor as mine. But common fate is of course a consolation.

The next day was a day off: an excursion had been arranged for the conference, with lots to eat and drink. I did not go along because I was waiting for my colleague. Instead I read the newspapers.

Through the newspapers I understood a little more. Not only had the speakers hailed the *Centro Luigi Severini*, which 'in this choice of subject [for the conference] had demonstrated the right qualities of imagination and courage'. The professor of jurisprudence mentioned earlier had also emphasised how the right to strike in his opinion was a 'fundamental right, but nevertheless a dangerous right, which—due to the many implications it has received in the modern machinery of society—as soon as possible requires a moderate but precise limiting regulation'. In other words, the professor held that the right to strike was too wide in Italy. I should of course have expected a professor of jurisprudence to be of this opinion. But I decided I would have to see how things developed, because I had understood that several of the foreigners were to talk the next day. Perhaps some of the foreigners, who knew Italian better than I, would discuss issues and problems in the professor's lecture?

When we entered the conference hall on the next day, conditions there were somewhat changed. Those with the gold and ribbons were not there. In other words, they had only come for the opening, and for the pictures in the newspapers. But some people were still sitting behind the '*Stampa*' sign.

An elderly venerable gentleman, who had been chairman on the first day, was chairman now as well. I understood that he was a famous judge from Venice. He opened by saying—this much Italian I understood—that an arrangement for translations had now been made, since there were so many foreigners present. A British and a French participant, who both also knew Italian, functioned as translators throughout the rest of the conference. They gave the most abridged translations of lectures and talks I have ever experienced.

Through some introductory remarks from the podium one issue was now clarified—a significant legal aspect of the right to strike in Italy at the time. Article 40 of the Italian constitution said that 'The right to strike is executed according to the legislation which regulates it'. For historical-political reasons, however, no further regulating legislation existed. The consequence was that the right to strike in Italy was unregulated though more detailed definitions of the concept of 'strike' etc. existed and were discussed.[1]

To me—and surely to many others at the conference—this was a quite sensational piece of information. There was, however, no time for further discussion and questions. Because now the famous judge from Venice began to call the foreigners to the podium, one by one, in the alphabetical order of their countries. They were asked to present their papers on the legal situation concerning strikes in their respective countries.

To a man—they were almost all men—they presented what they knew about the legal situation in their countries. A picture was formed: everyone who talked, talked of various degrees and types of *regulation* of the right to strike. When we came to the letter N, I thought I had better say something about Norway, and I presented myself at the podium. I emphasised the circumstances: in the first place, I followed my predecessors at the podium in presenting the legal situation, the law in force—I spoke about tariff agreements, the peace duty, arbitration, compulsory arbitration, and all of the other limitations and regulations. Secondly, I emphasised very strongly how the Italian Trade Union in my opinion ought not to follow the example of Norway and Scandinavia, but preserve their right to strike without restriction.

When I had finished, the applause broke out, especially from the large Italian delegation. Some cried 'Bravo!' Others threw their papers in the air from sheer enthusiasm. It was almost impossible to hear a word in all the noise. The chairman, the famous judge from Venice, thanked me smilingly in a lengthy eulogy. He had apparently never heard such an important and interesting speech.

Then I discovered what had happened. The first part of my talk—on the legal situation—had been translated in detail into Italian and French. But not the second—political—part. My strong warning against the Norwegian and the Scandinavian system had remained in English, which few understood. In the hubbub after the meeting the English translator explained to me that this was not law, 'and, you know, then the lawyers have a tendency to put our pens down'.

Myself, I did not put my pen down. I made the translators promise to give a translation of the second part the next morning. I prepared a written summary, which I gave them. The summary was translated correctly into Italian the next morning, but it was so early in the morning that few participants had arrived. When more people had arrived, the translation into French took place. The French-speaking translator emphasised very strongly that I had advised the Italian trade unions to *copy* the Norwegian system. I asked for the floor and said in desperation that this was exactly the opposite of what I had stated. But I necessarily had to say this in English. And it was not translated.

---

[1] I don't know whether this still is the case, but at any rate it was the situation at the time.

Through the rest of the day the presentations of the legal situation in the various countries continued, after 'N' in the alphabet. Everyone described limitations and regulations. And all the time the picture became clearer: the *purpose of the meeting was, through the presentations of the law in force in the various countries, to show the deviant character of the situation in Italy.* The purpose was well supported by the comfortable hotel, the good food and the rich wine. And that evening, the penultimate day of the conference, the news spread informally among the participants that the famous judge from Venice, the chairman, was to issue a summary of the meeting to the press, as president of the conference. It was quite clear what this summary would consist of: *an objective, and therefore impeccable, presentation of the law in force in the various countries, which as a sum would show—by implication—that Italy was a complete outsider in of her lack of regulations.*

That evening, my Norwegian colleague and I were deliberating what we could do. In traditional style from our work in the prisoners' organization at home we contacted other delegates whom we thought might want to protest against such a summary. But it wasn't easy, because the others pointed out—like the good lawyers they were—how could anyone really criticise a pure and simple presentation of the law in force? Never before had I seen so clearly precisely how an 'objective' presentation of the law in force is *in reality political.*

The last day came, and we were prepared to intervene: to ask why we were not allowed to see the president's summary. And we were a little lucky: a secretary had unofficially given the summary to an attorney who participated, a fact which produced very negative reactions from the judge from Venice, who strongly criticised the secretary as well as the attorney in a lengthy statement from the chairman's seat. *He* was to present the summary to us before releasing it to the press, we were told, but just in order that possible factual errors in the presentation of the legal situation in the various countries be corrected.

This gave us a chance to raise a point of order, something which normally was not easy. We said that we strongly regretted the procedure followed by the chairman, and emphasised that it was undemocratic that he alone should summarise the conference to the press. We held that a final communiqué either had to be drawn up by a committee chosen democratically by and among the participants, or not drawn up at all.

This was a lucky move, because the other participants also experienced the procedure as being diffusely undemocratic. Even more luckily, the famous judge from Venice argued strongly against the election of a committee. It was his task, as the president of the conference, to summarise the conference, he said. This gave us a chance to come back with still another statement about the importance of democracy.

And with this it all broke loose. A number of speakers asked for the floor and spoke all at once, in Italian, French, and English. No one functioned as chairman—the judge from Venice was largely preoccupied with making personal statements. Once, while the judge was talking in an especially loud voice, I waved my hand to be signed up on the list of speakers. The judge immediately interrupted himself and thundered that *he* had the floor now. The one who actually functioned as moderator was the technician who handled the tape-recorder: he could also give the individual participants 'sound' in their microphones, and the participants who got sound had a great advantage. So the idea was to point and gesticulate to him.

The famous judge from Venice now emphasised that he had actually planned to release the summary in his own name as president and not on the part of the conference. Therefore it was unnecessary for a congress decision on the issue. With that a part of the audience was swung his way—this was acceptable to many, they said. We pointed out—after being lucky enough to capture 'sound' from the technician—that the summary in any case would *appear* as a summary from the congress and not just from the president, and that there was a difference between giving a personal summary and doing it *as a president of the conference.* Personal summaries would be something we all could give, but the judge from Venice wanted to summarise *in the role as president.* At that the audience swung back to us. Once again we pointed out that either a democratically elected committee had to prepare a final communiqué and have it accepted by the audience, or no communiqué could be issued at all. We strongly advised the latter: no final communiqué from a congress like this. The result of the morning's session was, however, that a committee was established—with one participant from each country, chosen by the countries themselves.

I became Norwegian delegate in the committee. During the lunch break I prepared a proposal for a final communiqué, which said nothing except that the meeting had been 'informative' and that we did 'not wish to interfere in the strike situation in the individual countries'. A nice lady from the Italian broadcasting company helped me translate it into Italian, so that I could present it to the committee.

At the committee meeting it turned out that the Italian judges wished to be present with three delegates (but only one vote), 'since they were so many'. It was difficult to say anything to that. Then the question was raised of whether the judge from Venice should be able to be present and present his summary as a proposal to the committee. The judge himself did not wish to be present; it was said that his feelings were hurt. Several Italians pressed strongly for his being invited, and it was difficult to say anything to that either.

While someone went to look for the judge, I was asked to show the others my proposal. It was distributed, in English and Italian. A majority nodded approvingly; this was both straightforward and good. In came, however, the judge from Venice. First the judge did not want to read his summary, as far as I understood because it was—as he had said earlier—his own summary, not the summary of the conference. But he was urged to do so (not by me), and finally he read it—in Italian. In a couple of places he was stopped by those who knew Italian concerning corrections of factual errors in the presentations of the law in force in the various countries. The judge made careful notes—here everything was to be correct, this had of course been his intention all the time. When the reading was over, the majority nodded: this was both straightforward and good. The majority had been convinced that a presentation of the law in force simply is a presentation of the law in force, and nothing more.

The judge from Venice, and the other Italian judges at the meeting, had in other words won a victory in the committee. I, however, did not withdraw my proposal, but maintained that both proposals now had to be presented to the congress.

The last plenary session opened with an appeal from one of the organizers: he urged that this conference, like the 24 previous conferences at *Centro Luigi Severini*, should end in friendliness and compatibility. The judge from Venice now read—again from the chairman's seat—his four page summary, again in Italian, but this time with a 'sentence-by-sentence' translation into English and French. Finally it was possible to understand the details. It was clear indeed that here the law in force in the various countries was presented in such a way that a strong need for Italian regulations also became almost a logically necessary conclusion.

I was worried that the presentation would convince the plenary meeting, as it had convinced the committee. I waved to the technician, and as if by a miracle I got sound, so that I could make a statement right after the judge's presentation. I pointed out the actual political message contained in the summary, and presented my own—quite empty—proposal for a final communiqué. But I did not have particularly high hopes.

A certain development had, however, taken place during the afternoon. Turkey came out strongly and unexpectedly in favour of us: for some strange reason, Turkish delegates had been sent to the conference who were against any and all limitations on the right to strike. This gave us an opportunity once more to take the floor and say that when two whole delegations went against the summary of the Venetian judge, the judge ought, in the name of politeness, to withdraw it. And with this it broke loose once again: again people stood up or on their chairs and yelled and shouted. But this time there was more of a line in the yelling. The Swiss, the French and the Belgians came out as *opponents* of the summary of the Venetian judge. They had seen the political content in it. Most of them were probably in agreement with the Venice judge in his political view, but they were reluctant to be 'implicated in politics'.

And about there the conference ended. One of the organizers in despair tried a bit of legal dogmatics at the end: he distinguished between 'a congress' and 'a course', and emphasised that this was 'a course', whereby the president did not have to have his summary approved by the meeting. The distinction got little response in all the confusion. Finally the judge from Venice simply got up and left the meeting. The next day the papers—both the Roman papers and the local press—had write-ups about the lawyers' meeting which ended in chaos. 'Full disagreement among lawyers in Perugia', stated the headline in *La Nazione*. For the first time in 24 years, it was said, the *Centro Luigi Severini* had not been able to reach a final communiqué.

In other words, a happy ending. We had managed to stop an obvious attempt at using an international audience for political purposes. Before we left we even managed to pay our hotel bills with a travel grant we had received from elsewhere. The wine had turned sour.

What did we learn from this meeting?

In the first place we learned, more clearly than ever before, that the presentation of *the law in force contains a strong political potential*, hidden under a mantle of 'objectivity'. It is, among other things, through the seemingly neutral and purely technical presentation of the current legal situation that lawyers are able to function so politically, that is, conservatively.

Secondly, we learned, more clearly than ever before, how *difficult the unmasking of this political potential is*. It looks so plain and reliable when the law in force is 'simply' to be presented: a political stand is presumably not taken, we are only told what the situation 'is' today. In a subtle and suave, almost unrecognisable way we are silenced. At this conference we were lucky: the organizers handled the meeting in a tactlessly rough and undemocratic fashion, which people reacted to. With a more flexible and somewhat more 'democratic' procedure, among other things with an ordered sequence of speakers, I believe that the summary of the judge from Venice might have been accepted and adopted by the audience. This way the conference by contrast mirrored conditions in general in our Scandinavian societies: we have established precisely a 'democratic' framework for the functioning of the law; a framework which makes the presentation of the law in force easily pass as 'unpolitical'.

Thirdly we learned, even more clearly than before, how *important it is not to let silence prevail, and to unmask the actual political character of the law*. In Italy the political struggle is acute. Strong forces are interested in softening this struggle, and in subduing the opposition. As political people with a knowledge of the law it is of the utmost importance that we now spend time developing a strategy for unmasking the law. Some work is being done with a view toward this, but much remains.

In the fourth place, we learned that one must *prepare for conferences*. This time it ended well—through the newspaper write-ups we rather effectively managed to punch through the hidden political push. But we could easily simply have become hostages to the push. When choosing to attend, we should have prepared ourselves better, trying to have a larger group of like-minded people participate with us, and establishing contacts in some of the other countries. And this does not only hold for lawyers' meetings in Italy. At our own conferences, the lines are less clear and the goals more diffuse, but they are there, and precisely because they are less clear and more diffuse it is even more important to be prepared.

That is to say: we must continually think politically and be political.

8 Panopticon and Synopticon as Silencing Systems

CHAPTER 8

Panopticon and Synopticon as Silencing Systems

Michel Foucault's book on prisons and methods of discipline, entitled *Discipline and Punish* (English edition Penguin, London 1977), is a comprehensive analysis of significant aspects of the history and development of punishment. What follows is not in any way a review of the book in the regular sense, but a brief discussion of one theme which emanates from it.

I have said it in the English preface to this book, and repeat it here, toward the end of the book: what follows is not a denial of the fact that open criticism and protest exist in modern society. The great protests in recent years against aspects of globalisation are a case in point. What follows is, however, an ideal-type emphasis on the other side of the coin, a knowledge of which is now vitally necessary to an understanding of our society.

*

In 1997 I published an article entitled 'The Viewer Society: Michel Foucault's "Panopticon" Revisited'.[1] Very briefly, my assertions in that article were the following.

I discussed Foucault's emphasis, in *Discipline and Punish*, on a fundamental change and break which presumably occurred in the early 1800s from the social and theatrical arrangements of the past, in which *the many saw the few*, to the modern subtle disciplinary and surveillance activities of the present, in *which the few see and survey the many*. Using Jeremy Bentham's old formulation, Foucault referred to the latter as 'Panopticon', taken from the Greek words *pan*, meaning 'all' and *opticon*, which represents the visual. I maintained that Foucault contributed in an important way to our understanding of and sensitivity regarding modern disciplinary practices and, indeed, surveillance systems, which are expanding at an accelerating rate.

However, I also maintained that, surprisingly, Foucault overlooked an opposite process of great significance which has occurred simultaneously and at an equally accelerating rate: the mass media, and especially television, which to-day bring the many—literally sometimes hundreds of millions of people at the same time—with great force to see and admire the few. In contrast to Foucault's 'panoptical' process, I referred to the latter process as 'synoptical'; in contrast to his 'Panopticon', I referred to a 'Synopticon'—composed of the Greek words *syn* which stands for 'together' or 'at the same time', and *opticon*, which, again, has to do with the visual. I used this concept to represent the situation where a large number of people focus on something in common which is condensed.

Together, I maintained, the two processes situate us in a viewer society in a two-way and double sense. I explored the developmental parallels and relationships between Panopticon and Synopticon, as well as their reciprocal functions, and maintained that the control and discipline of the 'soul', or the way we think, is a task which is actually fulfilled by modern Synopticon, in the form of the mass media, whereas Foucault saw it as a function of Panopticon.

---

[1] *Theoretical Criminology* No. 2, 1997.

My article received favourable comments in professional circles. For details, the reader is referred to the 1997 article. Here I wish to highlight a major point which I overlooked or did not make explicit enough in the 1997 article.

Foucault's analysis of a transformation of modern society around 200 years ago, from a situation where the many see the few to a situation where the few see and supervise the many, essentially points to an important part of the development of *silent silencing*. I will give more more detail.

Assuming that Foucault's narrative is historically correct, we witnessed at that point a break, where modern surveillance methods of a hidden, unseen and silent kind, in which the few saw and supervised the many (in summary called Panopticon) came onto the scene. Of course we had had panoptical surveillance systems before the early 1800s—the Church, the Inquisition and the military are cases in point—but not on such a vast and rapidly growing scale, certainly not in such a hidden, unseen and silent form, and not in the form of gigantic electronic surveillance systems which came after Foucault but in line with his thinking. These latter include the *Schengen* information system, the *Sirène* exchange system, the Europol computer systems, the Eurodac fingerprint system, and the plans concerning communications control of telephone, mobile phones, fax, e-mail and Internet.[2] Presumably aimed at controlling terrorism and so-called organized crime, these surveillance systems end up becoming a threat to independent political opinion and freedom of expression, based as they are on highly vague and 'stretchable' concepts and rules, enabling the users to monitor wide categories of people, ethnic groups and whole nations, and, at that, just on the basis of hunches and more or less undocumented suspicions.

The modern panoptical devices, historically growing out of and to some extent relying on the mechanisms of internal prison control, are not only *silent*, they are silently *silencing* large groups of people and even populations. Those who are silenced are uneasy, unwilling or lack the courage to voice their opinions, to participate in demonstrations, to take part in rallies. In addition to being detained by the police, an open and noisy type of silencing which others

---

[2] For further details, see my *Siste ord er ikke sagt—Schengen og globaliseringen av kontroll* (Last Word is not Said—Schengen and the Globalisation of Control), Pax Forlag 2000, and my 'The Rise of the Surveillant State in Times of Globalisation', in Colin Sumner (ed.): *The Blackwell Companion to Criminology*, Blackwell Publishing 2004, pp. 437-451. For the most recent information, see Ben Hayes, 'From the Schengen Information System to SIS II and the Visa Information (VIS): The Proposals Explained', 2004, www.statewatch.org and in general net-based information from the British civil liberties' organization *Statewatch*. As of March 2003, the *Schengen* information system held records of close to 878,000 people and close to 390,000 aliases plus more than 15 million objects in the central database in Strasbourg (with 15 databases, one in each participating country, linked with and identical to the central database). As of March 2003 it had an estimated 125,000 access terminals scattered throughout Europe (figures from Ben Hayes). In the *Sirène* exchange of information (each of the countries participating in the *Schengen* information system has a '*Sirène*' office responsible for national administration), the *Sirène* offices may and do exchange almost any type of auxiliary information about individuals in any of the 15 countries. *Europol* has three large computer systems (a general information system where information about individuals is entered; a system of work files where over 50 types of more or less sensitive personal information, in some circumstances information on sexual matters, political and religious opinion, may be stored; and an index system). The *Eurodac* fingerprint system will eventually hold fingerprints and other information about virtually all asylum seekers in Europe, and the information will remain there for years. There are wide ranging *European and global plans to assemble traffic data* about telephoning, the use of mobiles, e-mail, fax and the Internet. And so on.

may see and consequently protest against, you may be caught in a web of noiseless, unseen, hidden, silent systems of silencing, which indeed lower your voice.

You may not be watched over by any of the systems; you know they are there but you cannot see them—they are silent—and you *don't know whether or not you are watched over by them.*[3] Perhaps you are watched all the time, perhaps you are watched at predictable intervals, perhaps you are watched at unpredictable intervals, perhaps you are not watched at all. At least if you are a politically active person, taking part in demonstrations and so on, you may begin to think in such terms. And you may end up by refraining from taking part and speaking up. That, in short, pinpoints the silencing potential of the silent systems of silencing.

*

But as I have said, there are two pillars—Panopticon and Synopticon. Increasingly, and again growing rapidly from the early 1800s on, there has been a development of the mass media—first the newspapers, then radio and films, finally television, first in black and white and then in colour, with an increasing technological proficiency closely allied with the technology of Panopticon, ending with a globalised and extremely rapid system allowing anyone and everyone to see a given event. The terrorist incident of 11 September 2001 is only one case in point.

The last building block is, of course, the Internet, which on the face of it is not a part of the synoptical system where a multitude gazes at a few stars, but rather a democratic system where everyone can participate in interaction, presumably on equal grounds. But in actual practice, the Internet becomes to a considerable extent a part of the synoptical system, in as much as it is, to a substantial degree, dominated by powerful economic agents—from newspapers and television agencies to owners having economic capital to invest in sales of lucrative merchandise, including pornography. To the same degree, the structure becomes characterised by a one-way flow, from the relatively few in control of economic capital, symbolic capital and technical know-how, to the many who are entertained or who buy the products.

To be sure, on the Internet the receivers of messages may choose between senders and may interact with those they choose as senders. They may choose between pornography, toothpaste, the *Daily Mirror* newspaper and the *Encyclopaedia Britannica*, and between types of pornography, types of toothpaste, specific articles in the *Daily Mirror* and specific entries in the *Encyclopaedia Britannica*. They may also interact with many senders, ask questions, obtain further information, state their likes and dislikes. But the receivers are still receivers, and react as receivers, not as independent senders of their own accord. Well, some of us certainly are independent senders: I have colleagues who have established their own home pages, hoping that many people will read what is on the home pages and perhaps react to them, even buy their books. But then others become receivers to them as senders.

A basic feature of the Internet is, in other words, that it constitutes *an interactive one-way medium, not an interactive two-way or multi-way medium.* The

---

[3] I owe this point to the Director of the Norwegian Data Supervisory Authority, Georg Apenes.

agenda is set by those with economic, symbolic or technical capital. There are certainly exceptions. Chat groups are exceptions. Games, played by two boys each sitting in his home, town or country, are perhaps exceptions, though someone has created the games and decided their parameters. So, deep down, hidden from sight, even the many games may be synoptical. At any rate, a large proportion of what you find on the Internet is. So is a vast amount of the 'information' you get on videos, DVDs and the like.[4]

*

The synoptical system is silently silencing, too. This is my major point here. The Internet and other ultramodern means of communication will not supplant television in the foreseeable future. Let me therefore, and also to be on the safe side, confine myself to the 'old' media, up to and including the most modern television.

We 'watch' television. In that sense, television is not hidden and out of sight, silent. On the contrary, it is there, in the middle of the living room. Lots of loud sound comes out of it. But television is endowed with a propaganda machinery which passes by us unnoticed, hidden and out of sight, silent: a propaganda machinery cloaked in entertainment. Nearly everything is entertaining on television. Out of sight are the conventional, conserving, conservative, uncritical and even reactionary messages, understanding and tacit assumptions which regularly come out of the television screen.

Of course, there are nuances. There are different channels, with different profiles. There are debates on serious issues where different opinions are presented. But the debates are also entertaining—parties are presented as polar and entertaining opposites. On television, even news telling us about extensive violence and war becomes 'entertaining', although we do not laugh. Indeed, television debates have turned into talk shows: Increasingly they have become huge entertainment exercises, titillating as we sit there, every evening, week after week, month after month, in an increasing number of hours. As a staff member of a large Norwegian television channel pointed out to me when I required greater nuances in a particular debate if I were to participate: 'But then we wouldn't produce television!'

In this sense, then, the influence of television is silent—as I have said, cloaked as it is in entertainment. And we are silenced by it. We are invited to share information provided by others, but on television (in contrast to the Internet) even the openings for replying are scarce, except in opinion polls after television talk shows and the like. In addition the entertaining slant makes it virtually impossible to speak up. In a sense, this would be to take things too seriously. Of course, we can comment to friends and colleagues after the show and during the lunch break the next day. But that is vastly different from participating actively and taking real part.

The most dangerous aspect is perhaps that we do not experience ourselves as silenced. In fact, the process is very satisfying. We like it. The silencing aspect is made invisible to us, —for the last time, cloaked as it is in entertainment.

Other media, including the newspapers, follow suit. The general trend of the newspapers, in competition with television and the Internet, is that of

---

[4] This perspective on the Internet is detailed in Mathiesen: *Industrisamfunn eller informasjonssamfunn—Innspill til belysning av den høymoderne tid* (Industrial Society or Information Society? Searchlight on the Age of High Modernity). Pax Forlag 1999.

tabloidisation, with large punchy headlines and pictures, short and sensational stories and simplified polarisation of viewpoints.

Is all entertainment evil? Of course not. Firstly, 'pure' entertainment is perfectly legitimate. Secondly, entertainment as a method of getting across important information and important political messages is also legitimate. Both the comedian Charlie Chaplin and the dramatist Dario Fo were entertainers. The danger point comes when the entertaining slant is transformed from being a means of presenting an important political message into being a goal in itself. That particular and fateful transformation has been an increasing occurrence over the years in the mass media.

The crux of the matter is the market. Media must sell, in order to live and in order to satisfy advertisers and consequently live better. It is cut throat competition.

Of course, what I have said here is well known.[5] What I want to emphasise is the *double* process of being silently silenced through Panopticon *and* Synopticon. Born in modern form at just about the same time; developing at about the same rate; both with particularly vigorous acceleration from the 1970s on; relying to a great extent on the same technology; the one (Panopticon) deeply hidden and out of sight, the other (Synopticon) protruding enough yet with a propaganda machinery which passes us by unnoticed; both with a great silencing potential— they both trail our silence in their wake.

The double-edged sword of being silenced through Panopticon *and* Synopticon is a fateful sword in our society. When you are frightened by the possibility of being in the watchful eye of the panoptical web, you can retreat into the safe haven of synoptical entertainment. It doesn't matter—live and let live. Probably no masterplan is behind it, but this is the way the two silencing pillars of modern society have developed.

Aspects of *1984* and *Brave New World* at the same time?

---

[5] See the much critised but important book by Neil Postman, *Amusing Ourselves to Death: Public Discourse in the Age of Show Business*, Methuen 1987. What I have said about the media in this essay is of course debatable. The points made are cast in bold relief. Mainstream media research advocates more cautious approaches. But in the mainstream research reports on the media main trends seem to be lost in all the cross-tabulations, controls and reservations. For a detailed discussion of the media and media research, with its strengths and weaknesses, see Thomas Mathiesen, *Makt og medier—en innføring i mediesosiologi* (Power and Media—An Introduction to Media Sociology), Pax Forlag 2002.

9   A Spiral of Silence?

CHAPTER 9

A Spiral Of Silence?[1]

In 1974, Elisabeth Noelle-Neumann published her famous and much discussed article 'The Spiral of Silence. A Theory of Public Opinion'.[2] Based on two important multi-subject opinion surveys taken in 1971/1972,[3] Noelle-Neumann advanced the theory that a spiral of silence develops in public space: voicing the opposite of the dominating (or seemingly dominating) opinion incurs the danger of isolation. You may become isolated, or believe you may be isolated, when you go against the opinion which is or seems to be the dominant one. Since most of us fear isolation, most of us become fearful and fall silent, not voicing our opposing opinion. When you are silent, the dominating or seemingly dominating opinion strengthens or seems to strengthen its position. As a consequence yet others fall silent, which strengthens the dominating opinion further, and so on. A spiral of silence is created.[4] Noelle-Neumann flatly states: 'To the individual, not isolating himself is more important than his own judgment. This appears to be a condition of life in human society; if it were otherwise, sufficient integration could not be achieved'.

Noelle-Neumann's theory of how a spiral of silence develops has been used in relation to the mass media and elections. The mass media are the most important source of knowledge about what goes on in the world. When a particular political view becomes dominating in the mass media, people with opposite opinions begin to hide their opinions, falling into silence. The more dominating the opinion in the mass media, the greater the silence among those who think otherwise. This feeds back into the mass media, further legitimising the dominance of media opinion. Again, a spiral of silence has been created.

Several criticisms have been raised against the spiral of silence theory. One criticism has been that media opinion is not always uniform. Opinions in the media are variable and in conflict, and consequently do not function as all that dominating. But in relation to certain issues there has been considerable agreement among the mainstream media. Examples from Norway are: a substantial agreement, from the 1950s onwards, on the importance of NATO membership; likewise, from the 1950s to the late 1980s, agreement on the need for staunch support of US policies against the then Soviet Union; from the 1980s onwards, the need for harsher criminal policies; and finally the need, especially in the 2000s, for a struggle to be mounted against terrorism to the extent that

---

[1]   Written in 2004, for this volume.

[2]   *Journal of Communication*, No. 2 1974 .

[3]   She also refers to classics like de Toqueville and Tönnies, Bryce and Allport, as well as experimental works by Asch and Milgram. The article was followed up in book form, including *inter alia* more recent opinion surveys; see her *Spiral of Silence. Public Opinion—Our Social Skin.* 2nd ed. The University of Chicago Press 1993.

[4]   This must be a correct understanding of Elisabeth Noelle-Neumann's notion of 'spiral' of silence; see her book (1993) p. 202 where she states,'[W]hen people feel that they are in the minority, they become cautious and silent, thus reinforcing the impression of weakness, until the apparently weaker side disappears completely except for a hard core that holds on to its previous values, or until the opinion becomes taboo.'

basic legal rights may be set aside. To be sure, on some of these issues there are exceptions and contrasting opinions to the predominant view,[5] but the degree of agreement has been or is great enough to make the mainstream opinion very dominating. And the agreement on some issues, for example on criminal policy, is so strong today (as opposed to the 1970s) that it almost reaches a 'taken-for-granted' level: It is taken as the 'obviously' correct stance on the issue; it is, as the phenomenologically oriented ethnomethodologists would have called it, 'common sense knowledge'.[6] Note also that the many television- and other media debates, which during this age of high modernity often feature substantial disagreements, actually for the most part focus on fringe issues or on areas at the fringes of important issues. To use Pierre Bourdieu's terminology,[7] the debates are frequently 'orthodox'—they keep inside the circle of officially accepted and acceptable disagreements on the issue without 'rocking the boat'—rather than 'heterodox'—where the debates dig deep into fundamental aspects. In addition, the heated 'debates' we often witness on television today, actually have entertainment rather than understanding and criticism as their main goal (see *Chapter 8*).

Another, to my mind more persuasive, criticism of Noelle-Neumann's thesis is that the two options of joining the dominant opinion on the one hand and isolation on the other are not the only alternatives. People do not stand naked and alone in relation to the media. People—including people who oppose the dominating opinion—belong to social groups and participate in networks of personal communication which may be supportive of oppositional opinions and which may soften the stigma of isolation.[8] In fact, people are inclined to seek groups as well as personal communication networks which are supportive of their opinions. The Norwegian EU referendum in 1972 (at that time actually an EF referendum, because the European Union was not established) is a case in point: Despite an almost universal and strong pro-EU membership for Norway in the mass media, the referendum went against membership. The situation during the referendum in 1994 was about the same—and the referendum again went against membership. Despite the dominating media and political opinion, the grass roots in the Norwegian rural and coast areas, where a majority voted against membership, had strong interests in keeping Norway outside the EU, and had strong social ties to each other, supporting each other in voicing the alternative opinion, if not in mainstream media public space, at least in the form of decisive and winning votes.

In other words, Elisabeth Noelle-Neumann's spiral of silence is dependent for its development on the level of participation in alternative networks and

---

[5] For example, from 1950 onwards a vocal minority opinion existed against Norwegian NATO membership. However, it was never able to influence opinion in the mainstream mass media. In 2002, and again in Norway, a disagreement over terrorist legislation, which had been proposed by the Ministry of Justice, between lawyers in very high public positions and the political establishment became public. The lawyers, while usually siding with the establishment, in this case emphasised the importance of civil rights. The disagreement was reflected in the mainstream media to some extent.

[6] See for example David Sudnow (ed.): *Studies in Social Interaction*, Free Press 1972.

[7] Pierre Bourdieu: *Outline of a Theory of Practice*, Cambridge University Press 1977.

[8] See for example Ragnar Waldahl: *Mediepåvirkning* (Media Influence), Ad Notam Gyldendal 1999.

personal communication. If the latter withers away, the spiral of silence has its chance.

In what direction does urbanised society, characterised by the features of high modernity so well described by Zygmunt Bauman as *liquid modernity*[9], move? Toward greater togetherness, participation in networks and personal communication? The signs are going the other way. In a recent book, Håkon Lorentzen (2004)[10] points *inter alia* to several strong forces which are developing and which may counteract a continuation of traditional Norwegian participation in local communal activities and communal civil society. Among these factors are *individualisation* and *market forces.*[11] Over recent decades, social bonds in a variety of social spheres have been weakened. To a much greater extent than before, the individual stands alone, and wants to stand alone, living his or her own life, reaching out for his or her goals. Market forces and marketability have entered nearly all spheres of life, particularly the mass media where they existed before but not to such a pervasive extent. Contracts have entered the social sphere where communal relations earlier were the order of the day.

Lorentzen is uncertain as to where the development goes. The future may show unexpected twists and turns. In any case, the more pervasive the corrosion of community, through individualism and market forces, the greater is the danger of a (media triggered) spiral of silence developing. Corrosion of community sentiments is certainly noticeable in political life, with faltering enthusiasm and dwindling concern with the empowerment of opposition. Even voting participation and party affiliation is decreasing. A spiral of silence in Noelle-Neumann's sense seems to be the political consequence.

*

Yet, I want to end on a brighter note. Political activism as well as ordinary political enthusiasm do still exist, functioning as buffers against the spiral of silence. And more may be done to increase such activism and enthusiasm. Individualisation and market forces are structural forces, and in the introduction to this book I referred to the silencing forces as structural. But this does not mean that we are unable to bring our influence to bear on them. Structures are, after all, dependent on compliance. They feed on compliance, or more correctly, they feed *on the belief that the only option is compliance.* As long as you believe that the only option is to comply, structures are strong forces. But compliance may be lifted through a concerted change of beliefs, followed by concerted action. Structures consequently change, and are at times even abolished. Max Weber's classical definition of 'power' comes to our aid here. He saw power as people's ability to carry out their own will in social life, and even if other participants in collective life were to resist it.[12] Weber's classical, intentional definition of power,

---

[9] Zygmunt Bauman: *Liquid Modernity,* Polity Press 2000; same author: *Liquid Love,* Polity Press 2003.

[10] *Fellesskapets fundament—Sivilsamfunnet og individualismen (The Foundation of Community—Civil Society and Individualism),* Pax Forlag 2004.

[11] Lorentzen also refers to the Norwegian social democratic tradition and the welfare state as guilty of a lack of understanding of civil society. Since World War II the Labour movement has, according to Lorentzen, formed a split between action on the one hand and morality on the other. In turn, this has strengthened the tendency toward professionalisation—the tendency of experts to invade and colonise civil society.

[12] Max Weber: *Makt og byråkrati* (Power and Bureaucracy), Norwegian collection Gyldendal 1971 p. 53.

often viewed as being from a ruler's perspective, is inherently optimistic and may just as well be used from below, from the point of view of those who are ruled. It contains the seed of another notion, that of 'counter-power'.

'Counter-power' is a fascinating but very complex issue. It contains a string of strategic as well as tactical considerations and choices. I once wrote a whole book about counter-power.[13] As a brief finale to this chapter and this book I will only give a short example. The example concerns penal policy. To repeat, the mainstream view on penal policy—and the need for harsher treatment—is very dominating indeed.

The key phrase is, in Norwegian *alternativ offentlighet*, in German *Alternative Öffentlichkeit*, as mentioned before (note 2 in *Chapter 6*), in English the much more cumbersome phrase 'alternative public arena'. The point is to contribute to the creation of an alternative public space in penal policy, where argumentation and principled thinking represent the dominant values. I envisage the development of an alternative public space in the area of penal policy as containing three ingredients.

Firstly, liberation from what I would call the absorbent power of the mass media, especially television. There is a widespread definition of the situation in the age of television showbusiness that our very existence as politically active individuals is dependent on media interest and 'media coverage'. Without media coverage, with silence in the media, I presumably do not exist, my organization does not exist, the meeting has not taken place. In Western society, it is probably impossible to refrain completely from media participation. But it is certainly possible to say 'no!' to the many talk shows and entertainment-like 'debates' which flood our various television channels, and, most importantly, it is certainly possible not to let the definition of our success and our very existence be dependent on our face being constantly on the television screen.

Secondly, a restoration of self-esteem and feelings of worth on the part of the grass roots movements. It is not true that the grass roots movements, emphasising network organization and solidarity at the bottom, have died out. What has happened is that with the development of the mass media which I have outlined, these movements have lost faith in themselves. An important example from fairly recent Norwegian history of the actual vitality of grass roots movements: In 1993, thousands of ordinary Norwegians participated in a widespread movement to give refugees from Kosovo-Albania long-term refuge in Norwegian churches throughout the country. The movement ended in a partial victory, in that all of the cases concerning Kosovo-Albanian refugees were reviewed by the Ministry of Justice. This example suggests that grass roots solidarity even with 'distant' groups like refugees did not die out with the Vietnam War.

Thirdly, a restoration of the feeling of responsibility on the part of intellectuals. I am thinking of artists, writers, scientists—and certainly social scientists. That responsibility should partly be directed toward a refusal to participate in mass media showbusiness. It should also partly be directed toward re-vitalisation of research taking the interests of common people as its starting point. This point is not new, but goes back, of course, several decades in Western

---

[13] *Makt og motmakt* (Power and Counter-Power), Pax Forlag 1982. Also published in Swedish and German.

intellectual history. The area is full of conflicts and problems, but they are not unsolvable. One important feature would be to produce greater public understanding of the fact that actual and potential victims of crime hardly gain anything from a hardening of the penal climate. Actual victims do not gain anything by the offender being placed in prison. Potential victims do not gain anything considering what we know about the lack of deterrent effect of imprisonment, especially the lack of effect following from stiffer sentences.[14] An increase in a wide range of resources for victims of crime would help the victims as well as ameliorate attitudes toward offenders.

We have attempted to combine these three ingredients in Norway, in the organization KROM, The Norwegian Prisoners' Organization, which is a strange hybrid of an organization, with intellectuals and many prisoners, with a common cause.[15] By organizing large conferences on penal policy every year (to create a tradition, organizing them in the same place, a mountain resort outside Oslo) with wide participation from the whole range of professions and agencies in the penal policy field and also many prisoners, by organizing regular seminars, and so on, we try to create *a network of opinion and information* crossing the formal and informal borderlines between segments of the relevant administrative and political systems. The point is precisely that of trying to create an alternative public space where argumentation and principled thinking are dominant values, a public space which in the end may compete with the superficial public space of the mass media.

Let me mention two points which may be to our advantage in trying to do this. First, in contrast to what goes on in the media, we try to work in the actual and organized relationships and networks between people. The public space of the mass media, and certainly television, is in that sense weak: It is to a large extent a public space which is disorganized, segmented, splintered into millions of unconnected individuals—this is its truly mass character—and equally segmented into thousands of individual media stars in the media sky. This is the Achilles' heel of the public space of the media, which we try to turn to our advantage.

Secondly, public opinion surveys consistently show that if representative samples of the population are presented with general questions about punishment, large majorities want stiffer sentences, but if the same or similar samples are presented with more detailed questions, providing context and background to given offences, their responses contain far more nuances.[16] This suggests that distance/nearness is a main dimension: The more people grasp of the context and background of a case, the more subtle and sensitive and the less harshly punitive their views become. Vivien Stern puts it this way (ibid. p. 315):

---

[14] See Andrew von Hirsch *et al.*: *Criminal Deterrence and Sentence Severity*, Hart Publishing 1999; Thomas Mathiesen: *Prison on Trial. A Critical Appraisal.* 2nd. Ed. Waterside Press 2000, pp. 55-84 and pp. 179-183;

[15] See Thomas Mathiesen: *The Politics of Abolition. Essays in Political Action Theory*, Martin Robertson 1974; same author: 'About KROM. Past—Present—Future', paper 1995/2000, obtainable at www.krom.no

[16] See Thomas Mathiesen: *Prison on Trial. A Critical Appraisal*, 2nd. ed. Waterside Press 2000, pp. 125-128; Vivien Stern: *A Sin against the Future: Imprisonment in the World*, Penguin Books 1998.

The research also shows that the more knowledge people are given and the more choices are presented to them, the more varied and thoughtful become their responses. As we have seen they usually say that in general the sentences passed by the courts are too soft. But when they are given the same information that the court was given when deciding on a particular sentence they are quite likely to accept the court's sentence as the right one.

Contextual and specific information suggests, then, that 'true' public opinion can contain many nuances. This gives hope for the future. Though counter forces are strong, it opens up the possibility of breaking the vicious circle of moral panics.

I have presented one line of thinking and working. There are obviously others. The curbing of our punitive climate requires them all. Similar ways of thinking can be used in other political areas of life. This is one way of breaking out of the equally vicious *spiral of silence*.

Bibliography

Aubert, Vilhelm *et. al.*: 'Akademikere i norsk samfunnsstruktur 1800-1950' (Academic Professions in Norwegian Social Structure 1800-1950), *Tidsskrift for samfunnsforskning* 1960.

Aubert, Vilhelm: *Rettens sosiale funksjon* (The Social Function of the Law), Universitetsforlaget 1976.

Bauman, Zygmunt: *Liquid Modernity*, Polity Press 2000.

Bauman, Zygmunt: *Liquid Love*, Polity Press 2003.

Beck, Ulrich: *World Risk Society*, Polity Press 1999.

Blau, Peter M. and W. Richard Scott: *Formal Organizations. A Comparative Approach*, Chandler Publishing 1962.

Bourdieu, Pierre: *Outline of a Theory of Practice*, Cambridge University Press 1977.

Brofoss, Knut and Ståle Eskeland, *Rett til arbeid?* (The Right to Work?), Institute for Sociology of Law, Oslo, mimeographed 1975.

Cavender, Gray: 'Media and Crime Policy: A Reconsideration of David Garland's *The Culture of Control*', *Punishment and Society* Vol. 6 No. 3 2004.

Cohen, Stanley: *States of Denial: Knowing about Atrocities and Suffering*, Polity Press 2001.

Dahl, Tove Stang: *Child Welfare and Social Defence*, Norwegian University Press 1985 (first edition in Norwegian 1978).

Ekeland, Anders and Thor Egil Braadland: 'STEP Arbeidsnotat, Notat utarbeidet etter oppdrag fra Statskonsult' (STEP Working Paper, Prepared for Statskonsult) Dec. 1999.

Embla (a Norwegian social work journal), No. 2, 2004 ('Subservient Social Workers').

En oversikt over departementets prosjektbevilgninger til forskning, forsøk og utredningsarbeid m.v. (A Review of Project Grants to Research, Experiments and Enquiries etc. from the Ministries), The Norwegian Research Council for Science and the Humanities 1977.

Endsjø, Dag Øistein: 'Skeivt i Disneyland' (Queer in Disneyland), *Klassekampen* 21 February 2004.

Etzioni, Amitai: *A Comparative Analysis of Complex Organizations*, The Free Press 1962.

Foucault, Michel: *Discipline and Punish*, Penguin 1977.

Garland, David: *The Culture of Control*, Oxford University Press 2001.

Goffman, Erving: *Asylums*, Doubleday 1961.

Habermas, Jürgen: *Strukturwandel der Öffentligkeit*, Luchterhand 1962.

Halvorsen, Knut: *Arbeid eller trygd?* (Work or Social Security?), Pax Forlag 1977.

Hammerslev, Ole: *Danish Judges in the Twentieth Century. A Socio-Legal Study*, Jurist- og Økonomforbundets Forlag 2003.

Hanisch, Ted: *Hele folket i arbeid* (Labour for All the People), Pax Forlag 1977.

Hanoa, Rolf: 'Utviklingen av sykefravær—sosiale og sosialmedisinske årsaker og konsekvenser' (The Development of Sick Leave—the Social and the Socio-Medical Causes and Consequences), *Sosial Trygd* 1977.

Hayes, Ben: 'From the Schengen Information System to SIS II and the Visa Information (VIS): The Proposals Explained', www.statewatch.org 2004.

Hedlund, Mary-Ann: 'Overvåkning—politisk disiplinering' (Surveillance—Political Silencing), *Hefte for Kritisk Juss* 1977.

Hegge, Per Egil: 'Arbeidsplasser på flyttefot' (Work Places on the Move), *Aftenposten* 2 March 2004.

Hernes, Tor: 'Myten om den rene og nøytrale forskning' (The Myth about Pure and Neutral Research), *Aftenposten* 7 March 2004.

Hirsch, Andrew von *et al.*: *Criminal Deterrence and Sentence Severity*, Hart Publishing 1999.

Ivås, Anne Marie: 'Yrkesundersøkelse for psykologer, statsvitere, sosiologer og etnografer i 1970' (An Occupational Study of Psychologists, Political Scientists, Sociologists, and Ethnographers in 1970), The Norwegian Research Council for Science and the Humanities 1973.

Jensen, Olav Irgens and Mons G. Rud: *Bruk av stoffer, alkohol og tobakk blant gutter og jenter i Oslo 1968-1976* (The Use of Drugs, Alcohol, and Tobacco among Boys and Girls in Oslo 1968-1976), Universitetsforlaget 1977.

Kobberstad, Tor: 'Arbeidsmuligheter for kandidater med juridisk og samfunnsvitenskapelig utdanning' (Labour Possibilities for Candidates with Legal or Social Scientific Training), The Norwegian Research Council for Science and the Humanities 1975.

Larsen, Terje Rød: 'Makt og herredømme' (Power and Domination), *Sosiologi i dag* 1975.

Larsen, Terje Rød: 'Hjerte og hjerne. Om den norske sosialøkonomiske profesjon' (Heart and Brain. On the Norwegian Economic Profession), Institute for Sociology of Law, Oslo, mimeographed 1976.

Lorentzen, Håkon: *Systemkrav og aktørtilpasning—en analyse av politiets arbeid i vegtransportsektoren* (System Demands and Actor Adjustments—An Analysis of Police Work in the Road Transport Sector), Universitetet i Oslo, magistergradsavhandling 1977.

Lorentzen, Håkon: *Fellesskapets fundament—Sivilsamfunnet og individualismen* (The Foundation of Community—Civil Society and Individualism), Pax Forlag 2004.

Lægreid, Per and Johan P. Olsen, *Byråkrati og beslutninger* (Bureaucracy and Decisions), Universitetsforlaget 1978.

Mandel, Ernest: *Innledning til marxismens ekonomiska teori* (Introduction to Marxist Economic Theory), Bo Caverfors 1969 (Swedish edition).

Mathiesen, Thomas: *The Politics of Abolition. Essays on Political Action Theory*, Martin Robertson 1974.

Mathiesen, Thomas: *Løsgjengerkrigen* (The Vagrancy War), Norsk Sosionomforbund 1975.

Mathiesen, Thomas: *Kriminalitet, straff og samfunn* (Crime, Punishment, and Society), Aschehoug 1978.

Mathiesen, Thomas: *Law, Society and Political Action*, Academic Press 1980.

Mathiesen, Thomas: *Makt og motmakt* (Power and Counterpower), Pax Forlag 1982 (also in Swedish and German).

Mathiesen, Thomas: 'About KROM. Past—Present—Future', paper 1995/2000, www.krom.no

Mathiesen, Thomas: 'The Viewer Society: Michel Foucault's 'Panopticon' Revisited', *Theoretical Criminology* 1997.

Mathiesen, Thomas: *Industrisamfunn eller informasjonssamfunn? Innspill til belysningav den høymoderne tid* (Industrial Society or Information Society? Searchlight on the Age of High Modernity), Pax Forlag 1999.

Mathiesen, Thomas: *Siste ord er ikke sagt—Schengen og globaliseringen av kontroll* (The Last Word is not Said—Schengen and the Globalisation of Control), Pax Forlag 2000.

Mathiesen, Thomas: *Prison on Trial. A Critical Appraisal*, 2nd ed. Waterside Press 2000.

Mathiesen, Thomas: 'Television, Public Space and Prison Population', *Punishment and Society*, Vol. 3 No. 1 2001.

Mathiesen, Thomas: *Makt og medier—En innføring i mediesosiologi* (Power and the Media—An Introduction to Media Sociology), Pax Forlag 2002.

Mathiesen, Thomas: 'The Rise of the Surveillant State in Times of Globalisation', in Colin Sumner (ed.): *Blackwell Companion to Criminology*, Blackwell Publishing 2004.

Noelle-Neumann, Elisabeth: 'The Spiral of Silence. A Theory of Public Opinion', *Journal of Communication*, 1974.

Noelle-Neumann, Elisabeth: *Spiral of Silence. Public Opinion—Our Social Skin*. 2nd ed. The University of Chicago Press 1993.

'Norske studentar og kandidatar' (Norwegian Students and Candidates), The Norwegian Research Council for Science and the Humanities 1977.

Papendorf, Knut: *Advokatens århundre? Globaliseringen og dens følger for advokatmarkedet* (The Century of the Advocate? Globalisation and its Consequences for the Advocates' Market), Report No. 47 from the Norwegian 'Power and Democracy Project' 2002.

Postman, Neil: *Amusing Ourselves to Death: Public Discourse in the Age of Show Business*, Methuen 1987.

Poulantzas, Nicos: *Politisk makt och sosiala klasser* (Political Power and Social Classes), Partisanförlag AB 1970 (Swedish edition).

Selznick, Philip: *TVA and the Grass Roots. A Study in the Sociology of Formal Organization*, University of California Press 1949.

Stern, Vivien: *A Sin Against the Future: Imprisonment in the World*, Penguin Books 1998.

Sudnow, David (ed.): *Studies in Social Interaction*, Free Press 1972.

Waldahl, Ragnar: *Mediepåvirkning* (Media Influence), Ad Notam Gyldendal 1999.

Weber, Max: *Makt og byråkrati* (Power and Bureaucracy), Norwegian collection, Gyldendal 1971.

Wendt, Kaja: *Ressursinnsatsen i samfunnsvitenskapelig forskning* (Resources to Research in the Social Sciences), Norsk institutt for studier av forskning og utdanning (NIFU), Skriftserie no. 29, 2001.

Index

By the same author

Prison On Trial

Thomas Mathiesen

The second edition of this widely acclaimed work. A book that distils the arguments for and against imprisonment in a readable, accessible and authoritative way - making the work a classic for students and other people concerned to understand the real issues involved in custodial sentences. As relevant today as when it was first published, arguably more so as policy-making becomes increasingly politicised and true opportunities to influence development diminish. Both 'an interesting read and a detailed analysis': Howard *Journal of Criminal Justice.* 2000 ISBN 1 872 870 86 6 Direct mail price £19.50

Black Women's Experiences of Criminal Justice

RACE, GENDER & CLASS: A DISCOURSE ON DISADVANTAGE

Ruth Chigwada-Bailey

This **second edition** of a classic text considers the multiple hazards of discrimination faced by black women on contact with the criminal justice process. This new and updated edition includes information about the many developments since 1997 when the first edition (reprinted many times) appeared. It includes first-hand impressions of black women of English criminal justice. Key reading on courses for practitioners and students alike. 2003 ISBN 1 872 870 52 X 160pp. Direct mail price £14.50.

Covert Policing

AN INTRODUCTION TO SURVEILLANCE LAW

Denis Clark

Covert policing allows law enforcement agencies to obtain evidence and information without the cooperation of the suspect. The practice has burgeoned in recent years, driven by new developments in policing. The technique is principally governed by the **Regulation of Investigatory Powers Act 2000.** This book is the perfect guide to the use of surveillance both human and technical, the interception of telephone and internet communications and the monitoring of financial or computerised transactions plus controversial data protection and exchange provisions and genetic monitoring. 2005 ISBN 1 904380 12 3 172pp. Direct mail price £16.50.

The Criminal Justice Act 2003

A GUIDE TO THE NEW PROCEDURES AND SENTENCING

Bryan Gibson (with Michael Watkins)

The ideal all-round treatment of the CJA 2003 and its impact across the criminal process. **Whatever else you read, you will value this clear and accessible introduction** which covers all the key aspects of the 2003 Act in a readable and accessible way. All the essentials: the keys to decoding 500 pages of statutory provisions - in just 172 pages! **Another Waterside Press 'best-seller'!** 2004 ISBN 1 904380 07 7. Outstanding value at just £16.50 (direct mail price).

Policing a Safe, Just and Tolerant Society

AN INTERNATIONAL MODEL FOR POLICING

Peter Villiers and Robert Adlam

This book bases its title on the UK Home Office motto: **'Building a Safe, Just and Tolerant Society'.** To build and sustain a society that is tolerant, safe and respects other fundamental principles is a key challenge of the modern era: and the theme of this book. From the authors of the acclaimed *Police Leadership in the 21st Century* (Waterside Press, 2003). With a **Foreword by Professor Conor Gearty** plus other highly expert contributions. 2004 ISBN 1 904380 09 3 160pp. Direct mail price £16.50.

Images of Incarceration

REPRESENTATIONS OF PRISON IN FILM AND TV DRAMA

David Wilson and Sean O'Sullivan

A thought-provoking work that examines fictional portrayals of imprisonment in order to provide challenging insights into **how popular culture affects public understanding of penal issues and hence influences penal policy via the democratic process.** '*Images of Incarceration* will appeal to criminologists, sociologists, penal reformers, media students and academics [etc.] . . . Recommended': *Scolag Legal Journal.* 2004 ISBN 1 904380 08 5 172pp. Direct mail price £16.50.

In Place of Rage and Violence

POEMS AND STORIES FROM WELFORD ROAD

Edited by Tim Reeves

Edited by HM Prison Leicester writer in residence **Tim Reeves.** Prisoners communicate their thoughts, experiences and feelings in their own words in a unique collection amassed by the editor during his two year stint at Welford Road. 2004 ISBN 1 904380 14 X. 80pp. Direct mail price £8.50.

The Criminal Jury Old and New

John Hostettler

An absorbing account of the jury from its origins to the present day (including post-CJA 2003). This book deals with the great **political and legal landmarks** to show how the jury evolved - and survived to become a key democratic institution. ISBN 1 904380 11 5. 2005. 168pp.Pre-publication direct mail price £14.50.